A RIDE
THROUGH ISLAM

A RIDE THROUGH ISLAM

BEING A JOURNEY THROUGH PERSIA AND AFGHANISTAN TO INDIA VIA MESHED, HERAT AND KANDAHAR

HIPPISLEY CUNLIFFE MARSH

GYAN

Published by

Gyan Publishing House
5, Ansari Road
Daryaganj, New Delhi-110002
Phone: 011-47034999, 9811692060
E-mail: books@gyanbooks.com

Distribution Network
gyanbooks.com
India, USA, Canada, UK, Australia, France

ISBN : 978-81-212-3955-4 (PB)
First Published, London, 1877

2nd Impression 2020

Printed at: Gyan Press, Delhi.

The book at your disposal is the edition of an old book originally published long back. The Text quality of this book may not be at par as compared to our other books but many readers approached us to reprint this important book so that it could satiate their hunger. We request all the readers of this book to help us to improve its quality by providing the necessary text of those pages which are not properly visible. Your valuable support in this case will be highly appreciated and acknowledged and our future readers will be benefitted immensely.

A RIDE THROUGH ISLAM:

BEING

A JOURNEY

THROUGH

PERSIA AND AFGHANISTAN TO INDIA,

VIÂ

MESHED, HERAT AND KANDAHAR.

BY

HIPPISLEY CUNLIFFE MARSH,

CAPTAIN 18TH BENGAL CAVALRY,

F.R.G.S.

LONDON:

TINSLEY BROTHERS, 8, CATHERINE STREET, STRAND.

1877.

PREFACE.

THE first notes from which the following pages have been written appeared in the *Allahabad Pioneer* in 1873, under the same title as at present. They are written from the journal kept *en route*. Although they contain very little, if any, addition to geographical knowledge, owing to my not having been able to carry any instruments, still I hope they may be received by all brother travellers, notwithstanding all defects, with the indulgence due to a first effort to add to the knowledge of a country interesting to most Englishmen. The matter from the columns of the *Pioneer* was subsequently printed as a pamphlet in 1874, which accounts for the Notes at the end.

LONDON, *July*, 1877.

CONTENTS.

A RIDE THROUGH ISLAM.

CONSTANTINOPLE TO POTI.

"Young" Turkey—Passengers on Board—Shores of Anatolia—Trebizond—Trade—Batoum—Golden Fleece of the Phasis.

THE Messageries steamer *Tage* from Syra introduced me for the second time to the oft-described beauties of the Dardanelles, Sea of Marmora, and Constantinople. As we swiftly floated along, all Nature seemed in repose—so quiet was the scene; very few sails glistened in contrast against the dark shore; those everlasting ten-armed windmills even were still. Just sixteen years ago, what a different scene I had before me, painted as it was in the vivid colours of my youthful imagination, and only slightly exaggerating the grand reality of that splendid panorama which is indelibly fixed in the minds of so many Englishmen. The Crimean War was the magical touch by which the whole country was illuminated. The bustle of Western Europe invaded the peaceful realms of the East, and imparted to fatalistic Islam that animation which so little suited it. The Bay of Scutari, with the old hospital and burial-ground to the right hand, and the domed and glittering pinnacled city to the left, were still in their remembered places. But what a change had come over the country. Nothing enlivened the scene, and the city appeared to have lost its splendour. On landing, everything seemed changed—for the better I must allow; but the street tramways did not seem to be in keeping with the traditions of the city. As it is not my intention to give an account of what is so well known already, let me proceed to notice only a few of the things that struck me most.

The Turk of the present age is a vastly different man to his long-robed, staid, and venerable forefathers. Now clad in the garments of the West, it is hardly possible in many cases to distinguish him from the Italian or Greek Levantines. In his religious duties, too, he shows great laxity; is beginning to look on the Frank as less of a dog than formerly.

But what shall I say of his sister, that mysterious "houri," whose charms used to be so carefully veiled from strangers' eyes? Now, one has only to go on the first or Galata Bridge, or Valley of Sweet Waters, and see their faces to his heart's content, for the finest of muslin now satisfies their ideas of propriety, and nothing but the latest-fashioned Paris boots gratifies their vanity, although white kids have no chance yet against henna-tinted palms. I did not see much beauty myself, but some pleasant faces only, and those nearly concealed by powder. After a week's stay spent entirely in sight seeing, I met a gentleman who had a mine at Yeni-Mali, sixteen miles up the Bosphorus. His offer to show me all he could was thankfully accepted, so early next morning saw us on the road; and after a two hours' gallop over a good road we sighted the pretty valley of Burkdéré, with its gigantic chinar or plane (*Platinos* in Turkish) tree, said to have sheltered Godfrey de Bouillon on his way to the Crusades about the twelfth century.

Having a beautiful view up and down the Bosphorus, this village is a favourite resort, and has many fine houses, all facing the sea; a mile beyond is Yeni-Mali. On the side of a white chalky hill, about a mile inland, is the copper mine, different to those in England, as we enter the galleries in the hillside at once instead of going down a shaft: the miners come from Trebizond, the Stamboulies being too lazy to work. Next morning we rode out to see the famous aqueduct and reservoirs at Belgrade. This is a most charming ride, along grassy glades in the cool shade; a little *café*, close at hand to refresh oneself in, adds to the pleasure. On returning home a swim in the bright clear waters of the Bosphorus refreshed us. After breakfast I returned to Stamboul in one of the many steamers that ply on these waters. She was entirely in charge of Levantines, the captain being a Turk and naval officer. Next day I got my passport *viséd* by the Russian and Persian Consuls: the former was very strict, with the latter it was quite a useless form, being only a mode of raising revenue.

Having taken my passage to Poti on the Black Sea by the Russian Steam Navigation steamer *Gunib*, I went on board in the evening, so as to secure a good berth, as priority of arrival gives one the choice. When on board I dismissed my man and caique, and turned to enjoy the witchery of the scene. The night was dark but clear, a slight breeze rippled the water, which reflected the fascinating panorama of bright stars and twinkling lights, and the lofty lighthouse of Topehana Point, off which we lay, formed one side of the frame, and the distant old Genoese watch-tower of Galata formed the other, of a *vignette* which was absolutely enchanting. Dome and minaret vied with tree and mast to shade the picture, lit up by lights from shore and sea. Far into the night I feasted on the lovely scene, which will not be easily effaced from my memory. We were to have sailed by midnight, but were delayed by the late arrival of the deck passengers. Poor wretches—Turk and Armenian, Greek and Albanian, Mogul and Tartar—in a confused mass, each strove to find a soft board on which to ensconce himself; and as these people always travel with all their belongings, beddings, baskets of food, bottles of water, bundles and packages of all sorts and shapes were soon covering the deck to such an extent that moving was impossible; so I dived down to the berth I had chosen, and thanked Heaven I was not as they were. The morning found us well into the Black Sea. The day being cloudy, with slight rain at times, made us all think that the sea had not belied its name, so dark and angry it looked, and by the evening we had a good tossing, to the discomfort of most on board. We were coasting the inhospitable shores of Anatolia, which looked savagely at us with its fringe of foam-beaten rocks, and badly would it have fared with us that day if we had been unable to "claw off" that dead lee-shore.

As it turned out, we were obliged to pass the towns of Ineboli and Sinope (of fearful memory for the Turk, who there lost a fine navy, destroyed by the Russians), being unable to approach their harbourless shores. As shipping cargo from open boats in such a sea was impossible, we were forced to go on to our next port of call, Samsoon, a small, ancient-looking place, fortified by high embattled walls on the seaside only, evidently for the benefit of their sea friends of olden times, when might was right. The shores are beautifully wooded, but cultivation is at its lowest ebb. Nevertheless, this place has a large export trade in tobacco, which is grown in the interior, and much esteemed as a light, mild, cigarette tobacco. This trade is generally in the hands of Greeks and Armenians, who have supplanted the Osmanli in his own land. The modern town extends down to the beach and up the hillside, but presents nothing of interest for the ordinary traveller. The deck passengers went ashore here, tired of their comfortless passage, the decks were washed, and a nice breeze favouring us from astern, we resumed our voyage with greater comfort.

This company being subsidised by the Russian Government, the latter employ their supernumerary naval officers as mates, to keep them in work. Our mate, an agreeable young fellow, together with the English engineer, did all they could to make me comfortable, unreservedly giving me every information I required.

Ordu being our next port, we were obliged to pass it without calling, the sea being still too rough; Kavassunde shared the same fate. The coast here is very pretty, being higher than that of the former place. The hills here rise to a greater elevation as they recede from the shore, and, being well cultivated by colonies of Greeks and Armenians, their ripening crops of barley and oilseeds give great promise of success in their undertaking. The port for this part of the country is Trebizond, and here at last I was able to land, but through a great swell. This anchorage is rather better protected than the others we had passed, as vessels find shelter behind a promontory that juts out. I went to call on Mr. Palgrave, our Consul (the Arabian traveller), but was sorry to find him absent; he had gone, as I was informed by the Consular dragoman, to Erzeroum, a distance of 140 to 150 miles in the interior. The dragoman being also a surgeon, finds plenty of employment, but was bemoaning the downfall of the town's former prosperity. Trebizond used to be the chief port for European goods imported into Persia, but since the Tiflis route has been opened goods have been sent that way, to the detriment of the trade here. The roads through Asia Minor are of the worst description. Caravans used to take twenty-eight or thirty days to get through to Teheran, viâ Tabriz; the couriers, or *cossids*, in about a fortnight's hard riding. The accommodation for travellers was of the rudest possible kind. Tabriz to Teheran, viâ Zungan and Casvin, is fourteen marches; Trebizond to Erzeroum, two and a half days; Erzeroum to Tabriz, eight days. The rate for posting is four and a half piastres per hour per horse: a piastre is worth twopence.

Notwithstanding the drawbacks to the route, large profits were made, and now thousands connected with trade will have to curse Russian enterprise. I had lunch at a small inn, on black bread and worse cheese, washed down with some wine, all home-made. While enjoying the above a young Greek came in, with gun and dog. He told me he had been out shooting for three or four hours, and got a brace of partridges, one quail, one plover, and one pigeon, all of which he drew out of his pockets to show me. Of course, there are no game laws here. Though there is plenty of cover for the game, next to nothing can be obtained near the coast, there being too many sportsmen, and all of the pot-hunting description. The population is of the usual mixed kind found in the Levant, but I heard of no Englishmen living there. On going on board again I had to pay an exorbitant fare for a few yards' row, boatmen being the same throughout the world.

We sailed again in the evening, leaving two steamers and several barques at anchor, dreading to face "rude Boreas" outside. We arrived at Batoum, an eleven hours' run, at 5 A.M. of the 29th August, 1872. A pretty place in a bay, with wooded hills to north-east, and small earthworks for artillery on each side of the village. This is the terminus of the

Russian Steam Navigation Company, and from here my steamer returned after a few days' stay. We brought up alongside a jetty, rudely constructed, to unload. A splendid harbour could easily be made here, but the general apathy of the Turkish Government is too great to think of such a "trifle." This is the only safe harbour on the south coast of the Black Sea. The Russian frontier is only ten or fifteen miles off. This frontier is rather troubled; the surrounding country is fertile, so that, considering this place in a political light, it is one of the most important that Turkey holds. The Russian Government are most anxious to get the district for themselves, and have offered Turkey a large sum for its purchase; but English politicians ought to regard Batoum with most jealous care; and as a strategical point against Russian encroachment and supremacy it could, by being fortified, play a rôle second to none in the Black Sea. Quarantine here is very strictly enforced by the Turkish Government, and is of the most vexatious sort, lasting ten days to a month, and that with the worst accommodation possible.

I went ashore to see the Consul for Poti, who, I heard, was here for his health, and found him in quarantine; and as I advanced to shake hands he begged me not to touch him, at the same time the soldier guard stepping between us—for if I had touched him I should have been detained also, if I had not paid a large *backsheesh* to the corrupt officials. Some of the British Consuls are a disgrace to our Foreign Office. Old, blind, decrepit, what chance have British subjects and interests in such men's hands against the wily Russians?* Before going further, I may as well give the proper timing between the ports on this line, as this is the terminus for the large steamers:—

Constantinople to Ineboli .	27¾ hours	Time:
Ineboli to Samsoon . . .	18 ,,	2 days
Samsoon to Ordu	8¾ ,,	18 hours.
Ordu to Kavassunde . . .	3 ,,	Fare.
Kavassunde to Trebizond .	7¾ ,,	2nd class,
Trebizond to Batoum . . .	11 ,,	120 frs.

I took from midnight of the 24th to 5 A.M. of the 29th, equal to four days five hours, owing to the bad weather.

The population of Batoum is a very mixed one—Armenians, Georgians, a few Turks and Circassians,

* See Note 1.

which latter have a small colony behind the village, being refugees from their own mountains on the other side of the border. With reference to these brave but unfortunate people, I hardly think Russia was wise in getting rid of them as she did. Nearly two millions of people were turned out of their homes, and literally sent adrift in the world to go where they could. Turkey has been a gainer by many thousands who, after many vicissitudes, have at last found a home to the south of the Danube. Thousands of waifs and strays have settled themselves, living on charity, throughout the surrounding countries. This place used to be a depôt for the walnut and boxwood trade, large quantities having been found on the adjoining hills; but, of course, European greed has killed the goose that laid the golden eggs, and little is left but her bones. The large rough blocks, portions of the trunk, used to be sent to, and find a ready sale in, Marseilles for veneering purposes. Though I went ashore, there was little to see, and the dirt and heat drove me on board again. At 4 P.M. we were relieved by seeing the paddle tug-boat that was to take us to Poti arrive and anchor close to us. Poti, in the Caucasus, is thirty miles from here, and is reached in this small tug-boat, as the bar at the mouth of the river has only five feet of water on it. She was on *pratique*, so there was no communication between us. All her passengers from Poti going on shore had to do quarantine. In the evening, I had a swim with the *Gunib's* naval mate in the bay, which was not over-pleasant, owing to the immense quantities of blubber fish that infested the place, and punished us severely with their sting. So many are there, that at times the shore is strewed with their dead bodies. Some practical man might, perhaps, bring them to account.

I had my last dinner on board the *Gunib,* which was a very cheerful one, as we had many visitors, such as merchants and the company's agents, from shore. We sat down to table, of eight different nationalities, able to converse in every dialect of Europe and Asia Minor, Persia, &c.; but, of course, French brought us on a level. Dinner over, I left them toasting "The Purees* of Stamboul!"

Collecting my traps, I got a boat to take me over to the tug. When alongside her I was going to step on board, but was roughly shoved off by her Russian

* Fairies.

mate, who asked me for my passport and ticket. But as no one understood French or Italian on deck, I was kept waiting for some time, tossing about alongside. Luckily, the captain of the tug spoke a little English, and looking at my papers, let me come on board. He with some Russian naval officers, bound our way, were having dinner on deck, but they paying no attention to me, I had to find my way down below myself, and take my traps too. There I found one large cabin with sofa beds, the 'tween decks very low, no washing place—a bucket doing duty instead. My only companion was a Frenchman, who I afterwards found out was going to Tabriz as Consul. Not getting any satisfaction out of him, as he would not speak, I turned in without supper, and in the morning when I awoke I found the cabin full of people who had come on board while I was asleep.

The tug had started at 4 A.M. (30th of August), and was out of sight of land, going across the Bight, opposite Fort St. Nikolia, distant twenty miles, and on the boundary line between Russia and Turkey. As this trip is only thirty miles long, we soon sighted the land again, off the mouth of the Rion. The coast is very low, reminding me of the Sandheads off

Calcutta. The roads here had six sailing ships at anchor, waiting for their cargoes, which go out to them in large barges when the weather suits. Dreary work it seemed tossing out there.

The first thing one sights off the mouth of the Rion is its white lighthouse; and as we approach nearer, the forest shows itself. The whole country is so low, that during the greater part of the year it is a dismal, dreary swamp, poisonous and impracticable, which, from the earliest time, must have presented the greatest difficulties to the trade of this river—the ancient "Phasis."

Would it be too far-fetched to recognise in its deadly miasma the veritable dragon of the Golden Fleece? The rivers are said to have gold in them, which is caught by woolly sheepskins, placed wool up in the river's bed, to catch the gold, and led Strabo to fable the Golden Fleece. The bar is shallow, with not more than five feet of water. As we went over its yellow waves it was at its deepest, the river being much swollen, and bringing down with it immense quantities of mud and driftwood. After steaming slowly up against the current, we arrived at Poti at 8.30 A.M., and made fast to the Government wharf.

POTI TO TIFLIS.

Passport—The Railway—Native Costumes—Quirella—Samavars and Vodki—Gori and its Ancient Dynasty.

NOW we were surrounded with all the signs of a newly-peopled country. The Custom-house wharf is of rudely-squared timber, as also the offices, and most of the houses are wooden.

After my passport had been duly examined, I was allowed to land my baggage, which was searched and passed out. My passport was kept, and instead of it I received a small slip of paper, with a number on it, by which I was to redeem it the next day at the police office, where it had to be registered, thus causing me to lose the train for that day. No one would sleep a night at Poti but for this delay; and I may as well state that before I left Baku I had four long *visas*, each one altering my name—the last leaving out my surname, and only giving my

Christian name. Of great use is this strict passport system, thought I. Going to the nearest hotel, which happened to be kept by a Frenchman (Jacquot), I left my traps in an uncomfortable-looking room, and took a stroll till lunch time.

There were a good many small craft that navigate the river lying along the quay, but not much business was doing—the whole place having a sleepy air. The bazaar was a busier scene, its small shops being kept mostly by Greeks and Armenians, and, though a Russian town, very few broad-capped Russians did I see. They have carriages here, with a pair of small ponies each, which can be hired, but at an exorbitant rate. I changed all the Turkish money I had left, and lost about ten per cent. in the transaction!

There is an old Genoese ruin here, of which I could obtain no information. Owing to the extreme unhealthiness of the place, only one Russian regiment is stationed here, with a small detachment of guns and Cossacks.

My landlord told me that, two years before, the site of the town I saw was a swamp, but by dint of draining and damming out the river, it was made habitable. All the public buildings are erected on piles, and foundations of large houses have to be most carefully constructed, to prevent them sinking into the bosom of mother-earth. Poti was taken by the Russians from Persia about the year 1828. The *cafés* at night were full of a most promiscuous crowd—many of whom are the English engineers, drivers, and navvies engaged in the construction of the railroad to Tiflis.

Ladies are very scarce at Poti. The few Government *employés* who have their wives here take them out driving in the evenings, to cheer the hearts of those who have none. Russian ladies, even in this out-of-the-way place, are never seen except *en grande tenue*.

Next morning I went to the different merchants' offices and money-changers, but no one would discount my circular notes. Travellers should be careful to obtain a sufficient quantity of Russian paper-money for first expenses, as foreign exchanges seem unknown here. Fearing to outrun the constable before reaching Tiflis, I left Poti the next morning at ten, crossing over the Rion river to the railway station on the other side, in a small paddle-steamer—one of the few that used to ply on the river before the railway was thought of At the station I found a crowd of people waiting for the only day train. These were mostly natives—Imritians and Mingrelians, with a few Caucasians and Europeans. The carriages are on the American principle, with a passage from end to end, clean and comfortable, the line having been opened to Quirella only, a month or so before I travelled by it.

The native costumes are not very striking. The usual one for men is a caftan or coat, close-fitting to the throat, with ample skirts; on the breast of the coat are worn the cartridge-cases, six on each side. These are made of metal, bone, or wood, and decorated according to the means of the owners. The cap is of sheepskin, with the wool outside, of all colours. The richest class wear it made of black felt, low in the crown and quite flat at the top. The waist-belt is of leather covered with metal studs and scales, with a buckle of some superior metal. Great ingenuity is displayed in the manufacture of these belts, and the design intricate. Sometimes they are of leather, covered with gold or silver lace; in that case the studs are few in number, and mostly star-shaped. To this belt is attached the knife or heavy dagger, in shape like an old Roman sword of Cæsar's time; the hilts and scabbards of these are a good opportunity for the display of their owners' wealth. I did not like their look, as they only dangle down in front, without being graceful. To complete the costume, a common straight-cut trouser and a shoe of half European make, without stockings.

The few native ladies I saw were dressed in ordinary European costumes, with the exception of a gold or silver band or coronet round the head, and over which is thrown a large veil, which hides the upper part of the person. This is seldom used to conceal the face, and generally hangs down behind. These bands show off to great advantage their dark hair, sallow complexions, and large features, of rather a Jewish type. Both sexes are fond of jewellery, and display heavy chains about the neck and waist.

We did not travel more than twenty miles an hour, and got to Quirella, 124 miles from Poti, at 4.30 P.M., having had lunch halfway. The country crossed over between Poti and Quirella is quite flat, a dense damp forest on both sides, reminding me of the monotonous scenery between Montreal and Quebec. The land began to rise as we reached the end of our journey, showing a few clearings and a miserable, listless race of peasants. Quirella is a most wretched little place of recent growth, its former native name being Zestipon—it has been changed to its present one by the Russians.

Thus ended my railway journey in a miserable hamlet, with a few boarded huts for shelter. The train went no further than this; and from here the ascent commenced of the spur of the Caucasus, which forms the watershed of the Caspian and Black Seas, separating the valleys of the Rion from that of the Koor. Here I was fated to remain three days, being the only one left of all the passengers who had started from Poti, which is accounted for, by all the better classes getting out at Kutais, the ancient Cytæ, a flourishing town in a wine-growing district, about six miles from the station. The hill on which it is situated is visible from the rail, but not the town; phaetons await the trains to take up travellers. It is the head-quarters of the Governor of Mingrelia, and the fashionable resort of all during the fever months from Poti. I was kindly helped by an Italian merchant who makes a precarious livelihood by acting as agent in forwarding merchandise on to Tiflis. He found me a room in a Greek *café* close at hand, in which I forced myself to sleep, it was of such an unpromising nature.

The traffic between this and the capital is carried on by large four-wheeled carts or waggons; they call them *fourgons;* to these are harnessed four horses, and are driven by Germans. They travel about twenty-five miles a day, and have no spring. Another mode of travelling for the poor is the *troika,* being only a washing-tub fastened to the cross-bar which connects the front and hind wheels, and the only spring is a bag of straw. For the rich is the *tarantas* an old-fashioned chariot, hung on four C-springs, and holds two, or at most three people. But as both these required a *padaroshna,** with which I was not provided, I could not avail myself of either mode, so I determined to wait for the diligence that was to start on Monday evening, and that only if it had enough passengers. In the meantime I tried to get off in a *fourgon* as far as Suram, the highest point of the ridge over which the railway goes, hoping to find means to proceed further from thence by the

* Police permission to travel by post.

trains that are ballasting the line; but unfortunately the German owner of the one I had engaged was robbed during the night of a part of his waggon load —a bag of sugar—and could not start in the evening as intended, so I had to pass two miserable nights on hard boards, having no bedding besides a couple of rugs.

This Poti-Tiflis railway was first proposed by Field-Marshal Prince Baratinsky, then lieutenant to the Czar in the Caucasus, in the year 1859, but was not completed till 1867 by his Highness the Grand Duke Michel. Of the section just finished the earthworks were principally made by soldiers, and the iron bridges by the English contractors, who also laid down the rails and furnished the rolling stock. Great credit is due to all concerned in completing this arduous undertaking—poisonous marshes at one end, and terrific mountains at the other. Near the Pass of Suram, for a distance of six or seven miles, the gradients are one in twenty-two, one of the steepest in the world. The finest part of the line consists in the ascent and descent of this Pass. The road plunges down valleys of great beauty in the basin of the Koor, the Cyrus of the ancients, and which is often invisible at the bottom of its deep bed. The engines used on the line are Fowler's double patent ones, of very great length and power.

On the evening of the 2nd Sept. I was rejoiced to find my former companion, the French Consul, also wanting a seat in the diligence; so, after paying seventeen roubles each, we at last started. The carriage held four inside and two in front in the *coupé* on the top; and by taking these latter seats we had a fine view of the country traversed. We had four small horses and a good road, so did the first part, to the beginning of the ascent, at a fine rate; but unfortunately it was a dark night, which sent us to sleep, and we lost the best view of the Pass, said to be 11,000 (?) feet high.

When we awoke at dawn we could see the plain before us—a vast stretch of yellow desert, which extends to Baku. At this spot was a post-house and we had our passports examined while changing horses. The road was barred by the swing beam, as in Austria—the sentry, in his long, brown-greyish coat, holding the cord in his hand, with his musket at the "order." The sentry-box was painted, as also the beam and posts, with the Russian black and white diagonal stripes. On receiving permission to start, we were allowed to pass by his letting go of the rope, and the beam rising of itself, being heavily weighted at the other end. As soon as we left the hills behind, our road lay through an uninteresting country, and our only comfort was having tea, as often as we could, at the different stages. The eternal *sumavar*, or Russian tea-urn, is always on the boil, and if strangers bring their own tea, they can get a refreshing cup; but if left to the poor Russians who keep the post-houses, the tea is generally strong and coarse. This, with black bread and *vodki*, a description of whisky distilled from rye, are the only things found ready *en route* at any halting-place. We generally had six or eight horses, each pair being driven by its owner, who rides the near horse. We were under the charge of a conductor in uniform, who was very dictatorial.

At 11 A.M. we approached Gori, the ancient residence of the Georgian princes, the last of whom was a general in the Russian service, and was killed at Borodino, if I remember correctly, in 1812. The Georgians are called by the Russians and Turks Goorjees, and their country Goorjistan. Though overrun and pillaged by Turks, Tartars, and Persians, it kept its independence and the semblance of a kingdom for two thousand years. They are, or rather were, the oldest reigning family in Christendom, dating from the eighth century. The last independent prince was Heraclius, who proclaimed himself King of Georgia, throwing off the Persian yoke of Kurreem Khan in 1791. In 1795 the Persian General Aga Mahomed Khan looted the capital, burning and destroying all he could, men and animals; but the son, George Heraclivitz, or Gurgin Khan,* not being able to defend himself from the foreigners, resigned his country to the Emperor of Russia, Paul I., his wife and family being sent to Moscow in 1799. According to ancient tradition, the founder of the dynasty was a certain audacious captain in the body-guard of the young and beautiful, but unmarried, queen. He was impertinent enough to take some very grave liberties with her Majesty while asleep (or supposed to be), for which he was ordered to be executed; but his sentence was commuted to being detached on divers hazardous services and adventures, managing

* As called by the Persians.

to survive which, her Majesty relented, and finally made him Prince Consort.

This quaint little town, with a rock-perched castle which commands the country for miles, is surrounded by low hills, dry and parched, which contract the valley; to a short distance on each side of the town the river Koor runs under the castle. Here we remained for a few minutes for breakfast, after which we went to see the antiquated church, the burial-place of former Georgian kings. We were only just back in time to take our seats. I really think they would have left us in the lurch sooner than wait. From Gori the road crosses several low spurs of the hills that enclose the valley on either side. In a hot sun, great glare, and quantities of dust, we galloped along, glad to reach Tiflis at 6 P.M., on the 3rd of September.

TIFLIS TO BAKU.

The Capital—Hunt for "Change"—Cabs—Bazaar—Our Vehicle —En route—Elizabethpol: its Wine—Nuka and Silk—Chemaka—High Wheels—Cost.

HAVING arrived at Tiflis, the capital of the Caucasus, and being deposited at the gates of the Government Post-Office, my next and most natural desire was to find out a hotel. The crowd around us was exclusively Russian, and no one understood French, so, after vain endeavours on the part of the French Consul to make himself understood, we started up the street, back towards a fine large palace we had passed, in the hope of finding some one who could understand us. The Russian gentry here, as a rule, speak French, but the middle and lower classes have no idea of any other language than their own; so also with the Georgians, though a few are now by force acquiring a knowledge of Russian. As soon as we entered the main street, we saw a large plate-glass fronted shop, which was unmistakably French. Having entered, the old lady at the counter kindly gave us all the information we wanted, and I soon had the pleasure of finding myself comfortably housed at the "Hotel Grand du Caucase Place d'Erivan, Maison Mirsoieff, tenu par Marius Martin." After enjoying a warm bath and dinner, I took a stroll around the square in which the hotel was situated. In the centre was a fine large theatre, around which, in the form of a verandah, was a well-lighted bazaar for small fancy articles. Then, all at once, I found myself in the midst of the principal rendezvous of the middle-class of Georgians. The women were mostly dressed in ordinary European attire; no trace of the native costume could I see, though the men still wore their favourite metallic girdle and dagger, but the cartridge-cases had given way to a frock-coat. The theatre, I am sorry to say, was shut, the season not having yet quite commenced. During the winter the town is crowded by Russians, when the Grand Duke and Baron Nicholi hold high Court the ceremonial being conducted in a style worthy of the Princely Viceroy to the Czar.

Next morning was passed in looking out for some

one to cash my circular notes. Going into the largest banking establishment, at first I found no one who spoke French, but a gentleman coming in, kindly explained what I required. To my great surprise, I was told that they did not transact foreign business, and they doubted if I should be able to find any one who would accommodate me. After calling at such places as I thought most likely, I gave up the search and returned to my hotel in despair, as I had applied to at least ten of the largest firms in the town. At the hotel *table d'hôte* I met two Englishmen, travelling for their amusement, and as we soon heard of one another, it was a great pleasure to meet countrymen and speak our own language again. By some extraordinary chance we had met, and found we were all going to the same place—Persia. They kindly asked me to join their party—an arrangement which I joyfully accepted, as a solitary journey in a strange land is not very pleasant.

In the evening we three sallied out for a stroll along the fine new street that leads to the palace and public gardens. Not many people were about, a high wind causing so much dust and heat that it was difficult to enjoy a pleasant walk. Nevertheless, there passed before us, as we sat on one of the garden seats to rest, a very interesting stream of people—Georgian ladies in semi-European dress; military officers in white summer uniform and flat white caps; Georgian servant-maids, or shopkeepers, in native costume, with ribbon coronets on their heads, and embroidered with silk and gold, long sleeves, and a veil thrown over all; Tartars in conical fur caps, shoes of raw hide laced up in front; Turks in long robes, in the white and green turbans of mollahs, mufti or priests; Europeans of all nations, but mostly Greeks, Italians, and Germans; a boys' school, dressed in a French uniform; lanky Persians, looking taller in their Astrakan hats; and Russian soldiers, bearded and stalwart. Water is very scarce, but a company, formed to supply it to the town, had just failed for want of support!

The best view of the capital is from the ruins of the old Turkish fortress above the Botanical Gardens. Twenty years ago it was a Persian town—streets unpaved, sludgy in wet weather, narrow alleys full of ancient and fish-like smells, and flat-roofed mud-houses; now it is a European city, handsomer and cleaner than many of them. This great result is due mainly to the Russian General Woronzoff, the founder of modern Tiflis, whose statue, surrounded by brass cannon, taken at Kars, stands at the foot of the fine bridge that crosses the river.

The next day I was in luck, for going down as a sort of forlorn hope to the offices of the Russian Steam Navigation Company, one of the directors, M. Petranowitch, very kindly offered to find out by the afternoon some one to accept my notes. In the meantime I took one of the cabs, a curious four-wheeled affair, with a driver who wore a large, shiny, black chimneypot hat, the top being broader than the brim!—with a coat that must have been copied from some antediluvian pattern. The upper part was double-breasted, with large brass buttons, and light-grey in colour: to this was attached a petticoat of a lighter colour, and fitting the waist by a multitude of gathers—a very curious get-up altogether. I went to the superintendent of the railway, an Englishman, but he could not help me, as the firm required all the cash they could collect to pay current expenses. Going back in the afternoon, M. Petranowitch did not disappoint me. He introduced me to a Greek-Armenian firm, Sowvarzoglu and Company, the head of which, M. Andre Gennady, very politely cashed my letters. This was a great relief to my mind, as I had come to my last rouble.

Though this is a new town, and has greatly been improved by the Russians of late, yet it is extraordinary to find such a difficulty in getting money for notes, which in Europe are as good as gold. After getting my money I drove to see a German colony on the other side of the river. This colony was established in 1810. It is a complete town in itself, each house having a considerable plot of vineyard and kitchen-garden ground attached. The cultivation is carefully attended to, and a great quantity of good wine produced yearly. besides the profits from vegetables and all sorts of European fruits, which are considerable. There is a solidly built church, an asylum for aged persons, an hospital, and sundry tea-gardens, spirit and beer shops, and places of amusement.

The new and old towns are divided by the river Koor, which flows below in a deep gorge, and is spanned by the iron bridge, from which there is a good view of he ancient city, five miles off, perched on the side o he adjacent hills. The Tartar bazaar was densely owded by natives, uncouth and unwashed, in rags, and with brutal heavy features, topped by great sheepskin caps. Their high cheek-bones, broad faces, and small slanting eyes, show their close affinity to the Mongol race. Greeks and Armenians generally outdo the Georgians in mercantile business, and have most of the trade to themselves. Georgia having been annexed to the Russian Empire at the beginning of the century, was promised seventy years' immunity from taxation, so that the present is a momentous period in the history of the country. The people have just been taxed for the first time in their lives on an equitable principle; and from all I could gather, the Russian army of ninety-six battalions, twenty squadrons, and sixteen batteries, at present in the Caucasus, is not too large a force to keep the country quiet, notwithstanding the skilful diplomacy of Baron Nicholi, the civil governor.

Having obtained my money, and the whole party being ready to start, we found ourselves on the road to Baku at dusk. From the hotel it took us half an hour to clear the town, which extends some distance along the road, the cottages being mostly of the poorest description, belonging to small gardeners and farmers, surrounded with orchards and vineyards.

The road being good we went along at full gallop, but did not go far the first night, and at midnight slept at a small post-house. Before next day's start let me describe the vehicle in which we were to travel so many versts, as we expected to be *en route* six days or more, according to the state of the roads.

The body was closed, and intended to carry four inside passengers; a covered *coupé* outside, behind the coach-box, held three, and the coach-box two—total, nine. The whole affair was on four wheels, all of the most massive construction, with the Imperial arms on the panels. Our party consisted of my two English companions and two interpreters—one a Greek, born in Constantinople, who thought himself a great traveller, but was a perfect impostor; the other, Joseph, was a Chaldean, educated by the French priests in his native village under the shadow of Mount Ararat; he turned out a perfect success, for a more willing, handy man could not have been found. With these two we spoke French; they both knew Turkish and Armenian besides. Our kit was not very large—a box of clothes each, a few rugs and blankets, a few stores, and our revolvers, completed the list. These things went on the top, covered with a tarpaulin. As travelling inside the carriage would have confined our view and cramped our legs, we chose the outside seat, which held us comfortably under its large leathern hood. Our Government conductor took his seat beside the coachman, and our gallant "protectors"—the Greek and Joseph—we put inside. We started at 7 A.M. of the 6th, along a good road; the country barren, with few inhabitants. As we proceeded, the Koor valley became broader, and the river lay in a channel not so deeply cut as at Tiflis. The distance to Baku is 510 versts, or nearly 400 miles. The whole day we saw very few villages, as the Georgians usually made their habitations under ground, as was noticed by Xenophon in his history of Cyrus's expedition into Persia.

Our papers were four in number, viz.—1. A general express *padaroshna*; 2. An extra letter, with the governor's official seal; 3. A letter to the post-masters *en route*, enjoining them to be civil and help us as much as possible; 4. A large sheet, with coupons attached, to be given in payment for horses furnished to us *en route*; and as we had paid "through" fare at Tiflis, these were to pay the local proprietors and contractors; but with this we had nothing to do, our conductor being responsible to Government. At each post-house they registered the number of our *padaroshna* and that of our conductor, so that there was a delay at each stage, of which we made use to stretch our legs and refresh ourselves with what we could get. The second day we fared badly, in having to drink some brackish water, which made us all ill for the day; food bad—black bread and old fowl; country growing more desolate, with no apparent villages—a vast plain in front, and distant yellow hills on each side. The fine military road which we had seen since leaving Poti is only finished up to here, and now, to add to our troubles, we had to proceed over a *kucha** road, such as Nature had provided. The horses were mere skeletons, and the stages long—one of twenty-five versts (a verst is about two-thirds of an English mile). We passed a Persian fort and bridge, both in ruins, having been destroyed by the Russians years before. In the evening the country began to improve, and in passing a small village we saw sheep, cattle, and poultry, but all in miserable condition. The fields had a greenish tinge, the crops having been cut only a few days before.

* Unmetalled.

More people were met on the road as we approached the town of Elizabethpol, which we entered at 10 P.M.

The post-house had some pretensions to being called an hotel, for it had a *café* attached. The *café* was full of stalwart Circassians and Georgian irregular cavalry officers—irregular cavalry are here called Cossacks--in full martial *tenue:* long black caftan, fitting without a wrinkle, and reaching nearly to the heels, girt in at the waist with silver-studded belt, from which depend an eighteen-inch silver-mounted pistol and dagger. Some carry a revolver in addition; a handsome falchion or sword, without a guard to the silver-mounted hilt, hangs from a well-arranged shoulder-belt, and a huge fur cap and a *bashlik*, or wide hood, complete the costume. Their overcoat is the Chakmen or Bournous cape, as worn also by the Circassian mountaineers. The glittering enchased silver of the arms and cartridge-cases forms an artistic contrast with the black dress, which is warlike without being gaudy. The senior officers had three or four medals, the Russian Government granting decorations freely for both civil and military service.

Next morning, before starting again, we had a stroll. The former or Georgian name of this town was "Guendje," and is of Tartar origin. The plain bordering the town was the site of a great fight betwee. the Russians and Persians in 1826, when the latter lost the last chance of recovering their former possessions in Georgia. In the centre of the town is a large "place," or *maidan;* with a row of fine shady chinars* all round. Here is held the market for fruit and vegetables, leather, &c., and all such articles as are not affected by thė sun. In the shade one sees the usual shops found in all Indian bazaars, and also one never seen in Asia—viz., the wine-shop; here the pure juice of the grape is to be had at all times. The wine being kept in large bullock hides, as in Greece, like the *mussuchs* of India, has a peculiar flavour from the skin; otherwise it is sharp and refreshing. We met a cart coming into the town with two large skins full of wine; the legs are cut off at the knee, which, sticking up and shaking with the motion of the cart, produced a most ludicrous effect. All the usual fruits of Europe were here in profusion; but the wonder is where they grow, as we saw no green spots or gardens *en route*

* Plane tree.

At one end of this *maidan* rise the lofty minars of a mosque, in a square fortified enclosure, the dome of which is decorated, in the usual Persian style, with coloured tiles.

Next day, on leaving this little oasis in the desert, we passed plantations of mulberries, both full-sized and dwarfed, as silk of a good quality is made here. Once past these, the desolate plain surrounded us again. On Sunday night (8th) we put up at a post-house on the banks of the Koor, at the principal ferry over the river in this district. A new bridge is being built, and in the meantime a ferry-boat is used, constructed to cross over along a rope by the force of the current alone, one man being sufficient to guide it. We delayed here for a short time in the morning to enjoy a swim; the river was very muddy, and the current strong in the middle. As we crossed over we found crowds of camels, loaded with bar-iron, waiting to be taken over; these bars come from the Volga and Baku for Tiflis.

We now diverged north from the high road to Baku, which follows the river some distance further, to go to the village of Nuka. Having crossed a low range of hills, we entered a valley parallel to that of the Koor, and passing along the same barren country we sighted Nuka on the southern and lower slopes of the Caucasus. It looked pretty, nestling in its groves of mulberry and orchards of peach trees. It is sixty versts off the main road, and used to be a favourite summer resort of former Wullees of Persia and Governors of Georgia. The village is built on the sloping side of a hill, with a southern aspect, and is the centre of a flourishing silk cultivation. I took sketches of the various machines used, which are very primitive. Georgian silk is said to have been of ancient renown, long before Italy ever heard of it, or made it a national industry. The reeling of the silk from the cocoon is done by one man, instead of two, as in Europe. While he is disengaging the ends with his hands over the hot-water boiler, his foot is at work treading a paddle, which causes the reel to revolve by means of a crank axle; the reel is gigantic, four or five times larger than Italian ones. The produce is very coarse generally; but a large factory, with the latest improvements, has been erected within the last few years by the enterprising Armenian merchant, Mirzioff, of Tiflis, who sends to market silk nearly as good as Italian. Every cottager has his mulberry patch, which causes the place to be well watered and cool; the water being brought into the place from a stream close by.

We went to see the old palace of the Persian governors. It is about 120 years old, and is tastefully decorated with coloured stucco in rich arabesque, of two stories, in a handsome garden, with fine chinars. The town is irregularly built; the main street, up a steep incline, leads to the Russian fort, which commands the place, the garrison of which is small—infantry, with a few guns. The caravanserais are large, roomy places, having small shops all round inside, for the sale of cloth, silk, &c. There are four of these, and each has an upper room or two fit for Europeans. The Caucasus produces wood of different species, but the trade in box and walnut is, or rather was (as the trade has died off, owing to the exhaustion of the material), the most important. The latter is confined to the *loupes*, or large, irregular knobs, which disease causes in the trunk. These are used extensively in Europe for veneering, as the pattern and grain of some of these *loupes*, cut transversely, are beautiful, and command a high rate in the French market.

Our quarters at the post-house not being very comfortable, we continued our journey the next day, and got back to the main road by the evening. At one of the post-houses we saw in a small pond a quantity of round, heavy hoops of wood soaking, and heard that they were to make the felloes to the wheels of the common country carts. The wood is some description of oak, cut as a sapling, bent into a circle while green, and matured in water. The felloe made in this manner in one piece is very strong and simple, which construction is being adopted in America.

At night we passed through Chemaka, the capital of the province—a large military cantonment. Unfortunately, we arrived so late that we saw nothing, and had to hurry on because of the want of room for us at the post-house, this being filled with officers. A few days before they had had a severe shock of earthquake, which had destroyed half the town. We saw a mass of ruins, and heard that many of the troops were under canvas. The place we slept at that night, Akchai, was the essence of disgust, and only fatigue, caused by the jolting on the road to Nuka and back, enabled us to get any sleep. Food we had none, and left early next morning—fasting, travelling, with six and eight horses, along the same kind of barren country. We arrived at Aksu by 2 P.M. The village being watered by a canal from a small stream from the hills, we found garden and shade, with a small Tartar bazaar. The only thing we procured here was fruit—melons, peaches, grapes—and Tartar cheese, like thick cream, preserved in skins, and very sour. Here we found the first trace of the wonderful natural production of Baku—viz., petroleum. The oil is used in large quantities for lighting purposes; the lamp is of red clay, like the letter "L" in shape, the top part being a receptacle for the oil, and the lower filled with refuse of cotton to form the wick. This gives a bad light, and dense smoke, and can only be used in the open air. Its advantages are cheapness, and that it requires a very strong wind to extinguish it; none but the poorest use it.

From this point the road leaves the plain of the Koor valley, and abruptly ascends a spur of the Caucasus. The ascent is steep from this side, requiring ten horses and a dozen howling Tartars to get us to the top. The hillside is nicely wooded, and when half way up we were offered some partridges and a pheasant by a *shikaree*,* who had just shot them in the jungle. From the top we were disappointed with the view—hot sun, thick haze, flat plain on one side, with a thread of a stream (the Koor) in the distance, and rugged bare hills and flat plateau on the other; general aspect sterile and uninhabited, with but a few green spots. Our descent on the other or northern side was hardly perceptible, as we advanced along a vast undulating plateau, with no trace of a made road. Travelling for fourteen hours, we only accomplished seventy-two miles.

It was not till 3 A.M. of the 11th that we arrived at a place where we could sleep. This proved to be a colony of that peculiar people the Malakans, whose creed is to mutilate themselves, lead a life of celibacy, and devote their whole energies to the worship of gold. This sect has been interdicted in Russia, and hundreds of them transported to Siberia, as in such a thinly-populated country as Russia the Government cannot afford to allow its subjects to live such lives. They make keen merchants, and understand currency

* Sportsman.

and exchange to perfection. They are tall, lank people, with German features, and with few social virtues. Here we had to find shelter, as it was raining hard, and the next post-house twenty miles off. The common room was full of travellers as we entered; three plank bedsteads, a *samavar*, with a basket of charcoal, its only furniture. We opened the windows to let in a little fresh air; on which we were attacked in several languages; and not till the people understood who we were, and were told by the conductor to remain quiet and give up the bedsteads to us, did we get any peace. They squatted on the floor with as much comfort as on the beds, and kept us awake for hours, making tea and talking to one another. Such filth as we found here could not be exceeded, and glad were we to start again the next morning, notwithstanding the rain. Crowds of women, half-naked, collected to see us off.

From this place we were only seventy versts from our destination. The road still kept up on the high ground that ends in the promontory at Baku, on which, though very arid-looking, we saw some flocks and herds feeding in the most likely places. The undulating character of the country is diversified by hillocks of red and white clay; rock does not show itself much, and all seemed water-worn, as if once the bed of the Caspian. The road was enlivened by strings of camels laden for the Tiflis market; and as we neared the sea the country became more open and flat, and, to our surprise, we saw carts. These are of curious construction—of wood, without any ironwork at all; the wheels are seven or eight feet high, fixed to the axle, which turns with the wheel, as railway wheels do; the body of the cart is then placed on the axle by two inverted wooden forks, in which the axle rotates. They are drawn by a single horse, and traverse the whole country without roads; and, owing to such a height of wheel, the draught is light.

At last, in the afternoon, we descried the blue line of the Caspian on the horizon, twenty versts distant. When yet five miles off we saw a carriage in the distance, escorted by cavalry; and, to our great pleasure, found it belonged to the Vice-Governor of the Caucasus, Baron Brügen. To this officer my companion had a letter of introduction from Baron Nicholi. He was rather astonished to see our eight-horsed vehicle draw up and ask him to stop; but on handing the letter he was very civil, and gave us a note to the police officer at Baku to look after us, as he was obliged to go in haste to some point of the Caucasus. His escort consisted of four ragged Cossacks on their starved ponies. By the evening we entered Baku and thundered over its rough roads to the only hotel it boasts of, Hôtel d'Italia; grateful again to see traces of civilisation, and get between clean sheets.

My expenses, all told, between Tiflis and Baku, were 93 roubles 5 francs ($1\frac{1}{4}$ rouble), or about 442 francs, and would have come to more had I been by myself.

Note.—33 pence = 1 rouble; 7 roubles 50 copecks = 1 pound.

BAKU TO TEHERAN.

Slavery—Virgin's Leap—Exchange—Petroleum—Steamers—Caspian Sea—Ashuradé—Land on Persian Soil—Ghîllan and Silk—Journey on Mules—Famine.

IN the morning the police-inspector came to see if we wanted anything, and shortly after the aide-de-camp to Baron Brügen called on us. This gentleman is engaged here in the difficult endeavour to put down domestic slavery. The Georgians, though Christians, and in common with all Mahomedans, look upon this institution as indispensable to their very existence, honoured by time as well as religion. It must not be confounded with slavery in the field, as practised in Cuba and Zanzibar at the present day, and formerly in the Southern States of America. A domestic slave is like a house-servant, born and bred in the family; though sometimes badly treated, he is on the whole well off, having every liberty and indulgence short of leaving his master. With the aide-de-camp we went out to see the town, built on the low sands, between two ranges of hills, at the mouth of a small stream. The main street has had to be reclaimed from the Caspian by a high sea wall. This road, formed in front of the best buildings in the town, is a modern improvement, and runs from one end of the town to the other. It has been substantially built, and has a breakwater of loose rocks, a few yards thick, in front of it, to ward off the constant attacks of the sea, which in rough weather washes clean over the wall on to the road. Half-way up this road is a large wooden jetty, for the use of shipping, which lie alongside of it. To the north is a dock and patent slip, worked by steam, for the repairs of Government men-of-war, of which there are several, of four and six guns, in the Caspian. The remains of a Persian palace, with its red stone Dewan-i-āmm* and mosque, repaid our visit. The former is now a Government store-house and magazine; from the minaret of the latter, built in 1660, we had a good view of the sea and interior. There are also near here, overlooking the sea, the remains of

* The public Hall.

an old fort, of which a tower of large dimensions and part of a curtain wall are all that now exist.

A legend is told of this tower, which goes by the name of the "Virgin's Leap." Some former Persian governor had a daughter, a strong-minded young lady, fit for the present generation, who refused to obey her papa, in marrying an old noble with great wealth, for which she was confined to this solitary tower to reflect over her naughty behaviour, her affectionate father hinting, that perhaps a little less food also, might agree with her better. One night the inhabitants of Baku were roused from their sleep by a lurid light illuminating the whole town. On looking for the cause, they beheld a startling sight On the top of the tower was a large flaming beacon, and attending it was the white-robed virgin. As they gathered to see it, they were surprised by a corresponding light flaming from the top of the adjacent hills, and the figure of a man in armour standing by it. As suddenly as the lights had been lit, so quickly were they extinguished. The father, on asking the reason, found that his dutiful daughter had a lover—and this was their mode of communicating; she having burnt her bedclothes, saturated with petroleum, he having lighted the gas which here exudes from the earth. After this demonstration on the virgin's part, the father remaining as obdurate as ever, the lover came by day under the tower in the guise of a fisherman. The girl, in the face of her father and his court, sprung over the parapet into her lover's arms—both were dashed to the ground, a great wave carrying their entwined bodies from the gaze of the world!

Baku boasts of a club and a small garden, all the soil of which was brought in boats from Lenkoran, on the coast. The streets in the new part are broad and clean; but the bazaar is poor and of ancient date; a new one, however, is in progress which, when constructed, will greatly beautify the town, the future of which will be grand, and when joined to Tiflis by rail will be "the port" *par excellence* of the Caspian. Next morning we bathed in the sea, the water of which is very much more salt than that of the Black Sea, notwithstanding the large rivers, Volga, Koor, Sufed Rood, Attrek, Emba, &c., are constantly pouring in vast quantities of fresh water. The Caspian, also, is rapidly drying up and shrinking into its bed, caused either by great evaporation or by the gradual rising of its shores. We changed some rouble notes for Persian silver currency and

Russian gold; the latter transaction was greatly against us, getting 400 roubles in half imperial pieces for 502 roubles paper. The afternoon was devoted to the great natural wonders of Baku—petroleum and the everlasting fires. We drove out in a carriage drawn by four ponies, across a desert country, a Cossack escort following us to Suleh Khanah. Here the whole country was saturated with petroleum; on making a hole in the ground a gas escapes, on lighting which, it burns for a very long while—one of the few spots on earth where this extra-ordinary phenomenon can be seen. When there is no wind the flame is dull and small, but in a gale it roars and leaps up eight to ten feet. The old Hindoo mud-built temple and cloisters, for the devotees who used to flock here as a place of pilgrimage, is a courtyard surrounded by small rooms. In the centre is a large Muth,* with a bell suspended in the centre, and from the floor rises the mouth of a small tube of iron, from which, if a light is applied, gas flames up, and can be extin-guished only by covering up the tube. This used to be a place of importance, but now its reputed sanctity has come to a low ebb. We only found one Brahmin here

* Shrine.

worshipping the sacred flames; he looked very much like one of our old Sepoys, but he stoutly denied it.

There are also two naphtha refining establishments, the furnaces of which are entirely heated by the natural gas, which is collected as it rises out of the ground in iron tanks, and laid on by pipes. At night the whole place is lighted in the same manner, by ordinary gas-burners attached to the walls. On returning home in the evening we saw the silent waste lit up by various fires, each surrounded by a group of wild Tartars cooking their food by its heat. The naphtha springs or wells are about five miles off, and the oil is brought in casks in the crude state as it is pumped out of the wells—a thick black fluid. The engine that works the Government patent "slip" uses this naphtha, instead of coal, for fuel. The oil is brought out of a tank by pipes, and is blown into the grate by the force of steam, the heat and flame being regulated with the same ease as a gas-lamp, and steam can be got up in the large furnace in a quarter of an hour.* This is cheap, and has the advantage of being clean and easy to manage.

In the evening our friend the aide-de-camp asked

* *See* Note 2.

us to dinner, after which he took us for a row in a man-of-war's boat to see the Naphtha Bay. It was a fine, calm night, and after a half-hour's row we entered a small bay, the surface of which was covered by a film of oil, which smelt strongly of naphtha; but we were disappointed in not getting it to light, a slight breeze having risen while reaching the place. On shore, which is quite uninhabited, is a small tomb on a low hill, and the old sheik buried here is said to have cursed the town in former years for its wickedness, saying—"Baku Bey," or, "May the winds blow on you for ever," from which it takes its name—and Baku is ever troubled by storms and tornadoes. The sea is called by the Tartars "Ca-Aspian," or, "Sea of the Horse-country," meaning Turkestan on the east coast towards Khiva. The streets of the town are paved with asphalte, which becomes soft in the great summer heats, but in winter is in excellent condition. Baku was first taken from the Persians by Russia, in 1805, when Prince Titiane was murdered. The general Zizianoff having taken all the country up to the river Aras (the boundary between Russia and Persia) was besieging Baku, after having defeated the Persians under Prince Abbas Mirza. The garrison, making overtures of capitulation, invited the Prince to a conference in a tent, and there treacherously assassinated him. The Prince's tomb adorns a square, which goes by his name. When here we feasted on the sturgeon, from the roe of which caviare is made; also on another fish of ancient renown—viz., sterlyat. History relates Nero having established a line of carriers from Astrakan to Rome, to supply his table with this dainty.

On Sunday evening we took leave of the kind aide-de-camp, after dining with him again, and went on board the steamer *Constantine*, lying off the pier. There are two lines of packets that ply on the Caspian—one for the Volga and North Caspian: the other for the South. The Volga line is stopped by ice in winter, when the river and shallow waters of the sea freeze; the southern line is always open. Before leaving I obtained from M. Zenovitch, the aide-de-camp, some old Georgian coins—silver. The one of Elizabethpol is inscribed in Persian, "Charam Khan of Ganja" (its former name), date 1220 Hijera,* A.D. 1703; and that of Nuka has "Ya Sabah Zeman," 1024 (Hijera).

At daylight of the 16th we passed some islands, and, shortly after, the mouth of the Koor at Salian,

* The Mahomedan era dates from the flight of the Prophet from Mecca to Medina.

where are established vast fisheries for sturgeon, which are driven by nets and boats into large staked enclosures, erected in shallow water, and killed with clubs. They often weigh 100 lbs. each. We were not very comfortable on board—no sheets or pillow-cases; food very coarse and badly cooked. We were only seven passengers—five men, one a Frenchman, agent to the firm of Ralli Brothers who lived at Resht, and two Russian ladies going to their father, the general commanding at Ashuradé. The coast we were passing was high and rocky, beautifully green—a great contrast to dry, yellow Baku. We called in at Lenkoran, a village on a low beach, backed by wooded hills.

The Caspian does not look like any other sea—all is so strange! No sail meets the eye—and few birds. The only languages on its shores are Russian and Turkish,* with a dash of Persian. One feels on a mysterious lake, with shore almost unknown. The bed of the sea is divided into two large basins by a reef of rocks that stretch across, occasionally showing themselves, from Baku to the Balkan; greatest depth about 500 fathoms. This great lake is entirely

* The Khivans and Turkomans speak this.

Russian, having been wholly ceded by Persia in the treaty of Turkmaneh in 1828.

Still coasting the land, we arrived off Enzeli, a Persian village on the Sufed Rood, 10 A.M. of the 17th; land low but well wooded, with the village close to the beach. The wind being from the north, there was a high surf over the bar; so we could not distinctly make the mouth of the river. Shortly after anchoring the surf-boats came alongside, and we hoped to be able to land; but were greatly disappointed by the captain saying the surf was too high to risk our lives—we must wait for another day. A passenger did come on board though—notwithstanding the captain's opinion—an American from Teheran. This gentleman I had met before in Cashmere, and now he was on his way to Europe.

As we steamed off again, leaving our port behind, our despair may be imagined. The sea got up during the night, and rolled us about cruelly. We passed Meshedesere, with its low, surf-beaten coast, without calling, and at noon had the pleasure of sighting the Ashuradé lightship. This island was taken from Persia in 1841.* Water very shoal, green in colour;

* *See* Note 3.

low, sandy shore to eastward. Anchored off the island to leeward. This is a small, low island of sand, covered with houses, with a few trees, and the head-quarters of the Russian fleet in the Caspian. We saw three corvettes, some hulks, and a small fleet of sailing ships at anchor; most of them were taking military stores to Krasnovodsk Bay, the starting-point of one of the Russian columns for Khiva. Many Russian officers came on board, and after dinner, while chatting over our wine and cigars, told us they hoped one day to take India from us, as it was their destiny to be paramount in Asia! just what they told Mignon in 1833, when they had taken Georgia. In the evening, we landed on the Persian coast at Kenagez, a small jungly village, thirty miles from Astrabad, the head-quarters of the Kajar tribe, of which the Shah is chief, and tried to learn if we could go overland to Teheran; but could discover nothing but that, if we would wait there for a few days, they would get mules for us from some place inland—and so had to return on board, a distance of about twelve miles, and not without a slight touch of jungle fever.

Next morning (19th) we were away again, back for Enzeli; the Elburz Mountains showing themselves above the coasts of Mazenderan and Ghillan. Gloomy weather did not improve our spirits, as we feared it would be too rough still for us to land. The mate, a German, told me that there was water communication from the Baltic to the Caspian, for small boats not drawing more than four feet, by canals, with locks eighty feet in length; but this was not generally known to yachtsmen. Next day, wind and sea going down cheered us, and we anchored off Enzeli again at 6 P.M. This time we were determined to land; so when the boats came alongside we got in with our traps, glad to leave the steamer with its dirt and bad food. The surf over the bar, which is about 500 yards broad, and about four feet deep, was not great; and we got through safe and dry, and landed on Persian soil at 8.30 P.M., 20th September, 1872

The village is sheltered by dense vegetation, and a feverish smell arose from the low muddy lake, said to be thirty-five miles long and twelve broad, in which we were. After taking some tea and a fowl, which the kind Frenchman got ready for us, we hired a boat to take us up the river Sufed to Pir-i-Bazar, which we reached at 5 A.M. The river is a sluggish reedy stream, with no traffic on it, although on the high road to the capital. Here we found horses for ourselves, and a cart for our servants and traps, and rode into Resht, a large town of 15,000 inhabitants, the capital of Ghillan. All here speak Ghillani, not a word of which could I understand.* All this time we were luckily under the wing of the French silk merchant, who kindly put us three up. Next day we called on the English (Abbott) and Russian Consuls, and walked through the bazaars, which are very much like the Indian ones. Here we saw traces of the frightful famine of 1871. We could obtain no post-horses to continue our journey, the famine having swept off such quantities of horses and cattle. The country is beautifully wooded, the wild hop growing in the jungle in great luxuriance. This province being a very large silk producer, about 900,000 lbs. a year, most of the trees were mulberry. At our host's house we saw some beautiful silk embroidery, done in the town by men—table and chair covers, cushions, stools, carpets, &c.—in all varieties of colour and shade. This he was going to send to the Vienna Exhibition. Next day, 24th September, after great exertions on our host's part, we secured six caravan mules, and started for Teheran, hoping to reach it in ten days. We were all provided with large goat-hair

* This dialect is very different from the ordinary Persian.

saddle-bags for our traps, on the top of which we put the saddles, we had brought with us, as best we could.

How thankful we were to be really off after such delay and anxiety. I took a large dose of quinine, being feverish, and fearing to become more so on crossing the swampy tract adjoining; the road was good over a large forest-covered plain.

The Persian telegraph between Teheran and Resht being worked entirely by natives, was festooned along the road, the wire being hung on any convenient tree or branch—without insulators! Our mules were pretty good, and the first day's journey was well got over, with the exception of heavy rain all day, through which we plodded. Getting up early next day we rode over the same plain, which ended in the afternoon, when we began to climb the rocky sides of the Elburz Mountains. Then, descending into the bed of the river Sufed Rood, the path followed it the whole way, up and down hill, the country getting more bare as we ascended. At Rustumabad we found cultivation; though a bare-looking country, crops of rice and maize were being cut.

This place commands a view of sea and plain. Here we began to lose the fever smell, and breathe freely again. Ripe mulberries in great quantities—large but watery. My companion caught another tortoise, which was small, but well marked. He had now three; each, having had a hole drilled through the edge of his shell, was fastened to the mules.*

The third day we entered a very hot, dusty, rocky tract, without a tree near the road, but there were a few solitary cypress trees on the opposite hill. At Rood Bagh, a pretty spot, we had an excellent lunch of meat, roasted in pieces on a stick—*kàbabs*, or, in Turkee, *shishliks*—with lots of grapes and melons, under a fine shade by a small stream, and passed through large olive groves in full bearing. The Persians do not understand how to preserve olives, and only make a very bad oil. There being no security in the country, no one likes to lay out money in machinery.

We reluctantly left the shade, and got again on the bare hill-side. After a night at Mendjïl, where we only had the bare mud floor of a ruined hut to sleep on, we arrived at the steep ascent close to the summit of the Pass. Near the top my mule ran away with me, and very nearly sent me over the cliffs; it was a

* Many varieties of land tortoise are found on the plains of Georgia and Persia.

providential escape. From the top we had a view of both sides—the plain towards Teheran bare and parched, that towards the sea green and hilly. The descent is very gradual, as the interior of Persia is a plateau 4000 feet higher than the sea. By the evening we neared Caswin, a large town, a former capital in A.D. 1600, in the time of Shah Abbas, who died in 1628 at Siri, chief town of Mezanderan, an adjoining province. The place is now in ruins; people miserably poor and half-starved.

There our mule journey ended—we had only hired the mules as far as this; and on asking for horses at the *Chupper-khana*,* found they had all died during the last year. We were soon surrounded by a crowd of beggars asking alms. Having some stale loaves from Resht with us, we cut off pieces and threw them amongst them, who fought savagely for each morsel. Mahomedans eating English-made bread at the hands of Kaffirs!—to such misery had they been reduced. We applied to the governor, one of the Shah's relations, Abdu Samad Mirza, or, El Khaneh, who kindly gave us fruit in his palace, and with the help

* Post-house.

of M. Natali, of the Indo-European Telegraph, we managed to get ponies, and started, passing through miles of vineyards, each enclosed with its wall. The condition of the *Chupper-khanas*, as we neared the capital, as also the road, became worse; the heat greater, the people more squalid, and the poor ponies mere bags of bone, falling frequently.

On the evening of the seventh day we found ourselves nearing the capital. A large canal was running parallel to the road, but the plain was treeless and desolate in the extreme. We saw several dry skeletons of travellers, who had died on the roadside, and been left to rot like animals. We passed a small walled village, where the people had eaten all their children in September, 1870.* This was told us by the people themselves. The snowy peak of Demavend, 21,000 feet high, on the left, and Teheran on the right, was a gladdening sight. We got into the city of the Shah-in-Shah at sunset; this city was entirely destroyed by the Afghans, but was rebuilt by Aga Mahomed about the commencement of this century.

* All the men who had the means had left the place, leaving only the women and children, and the mothers in their hunger stole and ate one another's babes, to save themselves from perishing.

CITY OF TEHERAN.

Defences—Hotel—The British Legation—Gulahek—Hospitality—Anecdotes of the Shah—British Influence—Coinage—Preparations for departure.

THE city does not show from far. Its walls, being all of mud, correspond so exactly with the colour of the ground, that it was some time before I could believe that the confused, dust-enshrouded mass before me was a city. The first thing we saw clearly was a large ditch, said to be four miles in length, which surrounds the city; the *débris* out of which—though traced on Vauban's system—had not been made into the proper slopes, but thrown up anyhow in a confused heap. This was dug prior to the famine of 1870, but deepened at the instigation of the English Committee for Famine Relief, who had 27,000*l.* sent from home, and to which the Shah-in-Shah Nusseeroodeen Hyder, Kajar, Sultan-ebn-e-Sultan (or a king and son of a king, as he delights to be called, although the dynasty of the Kajars only dates from 1794, when Aga Mahomed cruelly murdered the last of the old Zend dynasty, Lutf Ali Khan), contributed only about 300*l*.! and that after repeated solicitations!!

We entered by a gate on this ditch, which had a small minaret on each side of it, covered with blue and green glazed tiles, with a gold tracing over the whole. At a distance this gate looks well, but it is of the most tawdry description on close inspection. The ragged guard in pink! uniform tried to give us a salute, but failed, and the first thing that struck us, was a total absence of trees, except a few in the wall-enclosed gardens, that help to increase the size of the city. Everything had a dismal, deserted appearance—very few people in the streets—so that, with difficulty we found out where the only place they called a hotel was. This is situated in the European quarter, a good distance from the bazaars, but close to the new British Legation house and Telegraph Offices, also to the Champ de Mars. It is only an ordinary Persian house, taken by M. Provost, an enterprising Frenchman, who used to be the Shah's confectioner. You enter through a dark passage into a courtyard, with a small garden and water-tank—but alas! all was dry Out of this yard went the various bedrooms—small, close places. The walls were covered with stucco, mixed with pounded mica, which, when lighted up, gave a curious glitter to the walls.

There are about sixty Europeans in Teheran, connected with the British, French, and Russian Legations, Indo-European Telegraph, and a few officers in the Shah's army. Of Armenians not many are now left—they used to crowd here to trade, but found the Persians such sharp, acute customers, with large ideas and short purses, that they left in despair We then saw the city at its lowest depth of desolation and misery. The famine was certainly over, but the effect not yet counteracted by plenty. Everything was dear, the poor awfully gaunt and miserable, and all expected a winter of dreadful suffering when the melons and other cheap food went out of season. Next day our first difficulty was in getting any sort of animal to ride. So on two tottering ponies we started off to call on the officers of the Legation. Their summer residence is six miles out of town to the north, under an outer range of the Elburz Mountains, at a village called Gulahek, 3800 feet above the sea.

This village was given to the British Mission by Futteh Ali Shah about 1814 (shortly after the Treaty of Teheran, which was in force up to 1857, till we had to send an expedition up the Persian Gulf, because the Persians had attempted to take Herat). This pretty place is surrounded by gardens, watered by a *karaize* or watercourse from a succession of wells communicating underground, one with the other, dug on the slope of the hills above the village. On these *karaizes* or *khanats,* as the Afghans call them, depends the whole cultivation of the country, which is very arid and dry, with few rivers.

We called on the Chargé d'Affaires, Mr. Taylor, who has been here since 1853, my servant's former master Mr. Thompson, and Mr. Dickson the secretary; also on the engineer officer in charge of the Government Telegraph, Captain Pearson. Their houses are in fine large gardens, and they live in a very comfortable style. The latter officer very kindly asked us to come up and stay with him, to which we gladly agreed, as being shut up in a hot, pestilential city was not pleasant.

Here we spent many agreeable days, riding about the hill villages and valleys with our kind host and hostess,

The hills are very bare, except where there happens to be a spring, there the vegetation is luxurious.

We heard many curious stories of the Shah and his freaks. One day he became desirous of obtaining a Krupp gun, and applied to the Russian Legation to be allowed to get one from Russia. The Czar granted his request, and sent one of the largest and heaviest description—a 300-pounder. This was landed at Enzeli by a Russian man-of-war. The Shah sent a regiment to bring it up, but such was the difficulty of conveying an article of such ponderous proportions over a range of hills, without proper appliances and skilful direction, that brute force alone signally failed. After many months' delay and great expenditure of men, it was brought into the city in state, and parked with the other guns, and a day appointed to fire it. The whole court was assembled, together with a vast crowd, and the monster was fired. It happened to be so near one of the city gates, that the concussion knocked down one of its blue minarets, and the shot travelled so far along the plain that it struck a mosque in a village five miles off, and shattered it. The Shah, in dismay at the effects produced, had it put away out of sight for fear of more accidents.

Another anecdote. The French Ambassador was telling the Shah one day about the Cuirassiers with their polished breastplates. On hearing of this he also wanted to have a regiment of them in his army, and sent to France for 500 cuirasses. On their arrival, he formed a picked body of men to wear this cool dress, and said he would inspect them in a month's time As no commanding officer had been appointed, this gallant corps knew they would get no pay—as the commanding officer pays the men; so they deserted in a mass, a few days before the regal inspection. The Sudr Azan, or Prime Minister knowing his master, had 500 coolies or hamals from the bazaar collected and dressed up in them. All looked perfect to outward appearance, having been beaten into line and order. The Shah was greatly pleased at the show, and determined to mount them, and asked his brave armv if they had any request to make. To the Wuzeer's horror, the whole body ran pell mell, and threw themselves at the Shah's feet, and prayed that the Sudr Azan might be prevented from enlisting them for any such work for the future!

Then he must establish a Royal Mint, and spend thousands in buildings and plant, which, in a state of neglect and rust, are a monument to his folly to this day. He has several palaces round about the city, tawdry but not grand. He also wished to make a road over the mountains to the sea coast at Meshedirissa, a work which would have been of real use, but was opposed by the Governor of Mazenderan,* who was jealous of any encroachments on his inaccesible province from the side of the capital. The Shah is fond of a variety of uniforms, as also of colours. The soldiers' uniform being of cotton, though of European cut, he has only to put the coats in the dye-tub to change entirely the appearance of a regiment. For instance, the pink regiment I saw on duty at the gates will some day be green, and those now in white in some other colour.

The troops ape European drill, and have grand field-days in the large walled enclosure near the Embassy. I saw four regiments together marching past, under the command of General Buhles, in gorgeous war-paint, who was at the taking of Herat in 1856—a Frenchman by birth. The plan seems to be, to have a few men with sticks, who understand their

* A province on the Caspian.

drill, independent of the officers of the regiment, who smarten slackness or delay in moving, from behind. Some of the Shah's guns are good. I saw six brass 9- or 12-pounder muzzle-loading rifled guns that had been lately cast, and which, with their carriages, seemed serviceable weapons. The troops are very strong on paper, but I doubt if a force could be collected of 15,000 men, for any emergency. They are armed with old smooth-bores, and some with flint locks. Their bands are a great institution, and of which they are very proud; but I leave you to imagine the "melody" I used to hear while passing the Nobut-khanah, or music-room.

The influence of the different embassies at the Shah's court entirely depends on the ambassadors personally. The Russians being able to coerce, and doing so freely, are of course the favoured nation; and through them, I believe, was granted the establishment of a line of railway from Resht to Teheran, and eventually to Bushire, the firm being the great speculator, Baron Reuter. From all I could learn, our influence has of late been *nil.* They understood our system of patting on the back (and thanks to the conduct of a late ambassador, a man of no good repute, and of no personal influence with the Shah), so that we are at a low ebb in point of consideration with the people and the court. The appointments to this mission ought to be for a limited tenure, for men of English blood and birth only, otherwise they become small-minded, and influenced by personal considerations.

The Persians are proud of their nationality—nearly the same race as the ancient Medes, a branch of the great Aryan stock, which, under various names, established their sway over the whole country between the Euphrates and Bramapootra. They still retain some few of the characteristics of their ancestors—good horsemen, fond of display, physically strong, of a hardy temperament, but remarkable for their servile bearing and the abject flattery of their rulers. Of late years the nation has lost its reputation for courage, and is no match in equal numbers to their neighbours the Afghans. They are great liars; deceit is regarded by them nowadays as a thing not only to be inherited, but studiously cultivated. I am sorry I had not the honour of seeing the Lord of the Lion and the Sun: he was ill during my stay. His late visit to Europe will, I am afraid, not produce many good effects. As long as he is an irresponsible autocrat, so long will poor Persia groan at the rapacity of its ruler.

Here again I had the same difficulty of getting my circular notes changed into krans, as I had in Tiflis into roubles; but luckily the British Consul was about to leave the country, and we each wanted what the other had. The coinage of the country is generally silver. The toman=11·20 frs.;* the kran=1·10 fr.; 20 shaie (of copper)=1 kran; 10 krans (silver)=1 toman, tilla, or ashurfee of gold. I had two large bags of krans, which were difficult to carry owing to their weight; and as I was not able to obtain all the gold I required, which was at a high premium, I had to accept silver.

As I intended to return to India overland my movements were regulated by the fact that between this and Meshed there is danger of being attacked by the Turkomans. The *zowars*† to that holy city were escorted twice a month by a gun and a few mounted men; and I wished to time myself so as to take advantage of this *kafila*. I got no help from the

* About eight shillings and ninepence.

† Pilgrims.

British Embassy, except a note to our Persian agent at Meshed; in fact, the Chargé d'Affaires tried to dissuade me from going, and so did all. I could get no information about the road, or of the state of the country at Herat. The last thing I heard was a rumour at the Legation, that Surdar Abdool Rahman, son of ex-Ameer Afzul Khan and cousin to the Ameer Shere Ali, had taken Balkh from the Bokhara side, and was strengthening himself for a *chuppau** on Herat! Two days before my departure, I left my kind friends and went back to the city. My travelling companions and I parted—one to Tabriz; one to Shiraz; and self to Herat: north, south and east.

As all my future travelling was to be done on horseback over bad roads, I exchanged my small portmanteau for another pair of saddle-bags. I provided myself with a servant, a kettle, sugar and tea, candles, &c.—all on the smallest scale. All I possessed was to go into four small bags, and my rug for bedding, on my saddle. The day before I started, the Velayet, or heir apparent, the Shah's third son Muzuffer-o-deen Mirza, arrived from Tabriz, and was received

* Raid.

with honours. He seems to be popular; and is intended to take the Shah's place when he goes on his European tour. I hope Nusseeroodeen wont find himself without a throne on his return—which is his great fear. I obtained my *tushkereh*, or permission to travel, with great difficulty and delay. I was to go by chupper, or post, as far as Meshed.

Next morning, on going for the horses, I went for the last time through the great vaulted bazaar of Abbas Shah, and beheld the fearful misery from starvation on all sides; and fearing to get nothing myself *en route*, added two pots of Liebig's soup* to my kit. The crowds round the butchers' and fruitsellers' stalls were pitiable; all eagerly looking out for any morsel of offal or rotten fruit that might be thrown away, and which would be fought for and eagerly devoured.

The last evening, as I sat all alone, I felt much depressed at my future—which was a direct sin against that merciful Providence who watched over me.

* This I found most refreshing at times in lieu of tea.

TEHERAN TO MESHED.

Commence my *Chappar* Ride—Semnoon—The Gun Escort—Sharood; its Armenians and Bazaars—The Russian—Solitary Travelling—Subzewar—Singing Boy—Sportsmen—Enter the Holy City.

ON the 17th, early, I rode out of Teheran, with my servant behind shouting *Hosh!* and *Kubardar!** to clear a road through the crowd. Once more was I launched on the sea of uncertainty, and steered by the rudder of hope. As I rode out of the outer gate, I looked back with a sort of regret at the last European link behind me; but was glad to quit the city with its depressing sights. As we, servant and I, galloped along, with a few undulating hills ahead of us, and the village of Shah Abdool Azin, with its glittering mosque, four miles off to the right, we saw during the first stage many old brick ruins, such as tombs, serais, &c., and several large, walled enclosures quite deserted. In former days these used

* "Have a care."

to be full of cattle; but now all are dead and gone—nothing remains but large heaps of bones. We slept at Ewan-i-Keef (thirty-six miles) the first night.

Next morning we rode into a *cul-de-sac* between two hills—the country being all a hard salt desert. The path was so badly marked, that if we had not met some *shuterwans,* or camel-drivers, who were grazing their animals here on a prickly green bush that abounded, we should have lost our way, which lay along the side of a salt stream, the banks of which were quite white with its incrustations. We were very thirsty; but not even our sorry nags would touch the water—so bitter was it.

The second night we arrived at Deynemak, or Salt Village, having passed some canals of bitter water and the ruins of two large mud forts. The earth out of which they are built is so tenacious that, though the people say they have been in ruins more than a hundred years, they are still in a tolerable state, and it would not take much to make them defensible again. Such is the facility of entrenching oneself, that in former days, and more or less now, towers and forts rise like magic whenever a district becomes *yaghy,* or rebellious.

Lashgird we reached at noon, and were glad of the shelter its gardens afforded. This is a most curious village, being built on a tower of vast dimensions, or rather the tower itself was the village. At an elevation of fifty or sixty feet, the houses are built in three stories, or rings, facing outwards, and to each story is a large verandah or balcony, formed of poles built into the tower, the lower verandah forming the passage into the house above, so on to the top—a most curious arrangement. The door into the base of the tower is about twenty feet above the ground. A mud staircase leads up, which on the approach of a hostile force is cut away, leaving the door in mid-air; and when the Government is weak, it has to send out a force with the tax-gatherer to enable him to collect the Government dues.

Semnoon came next, with its green-tiled musjids, and a minar of most elegant construction, very lofty and slender. There are also large ruins of a palace begun by Abbas Sheik. Its bazaar is a large one, well-walled: and both on approaching and leaving the town one has to pass through miles of gardens. The province of Khorasan begins here. This place boasts of a governor, and is a very pretty village on a spur of the

Elburz, and was in former days a very thriving one; now hardly one thousand inhabitants are left.

Afraid of being too late for the gun escort, I had to push on, and reluctantly left this pretty spot at 7 P.M. for another stage. Moonlit as it was, the road was a difficult one, leading over a hilly track quite deserted; so when we arrived at the solitary post-house and serai of Ahoowan at 1 A.M., it was after much knocking and abuse on the part of my man that we managed to obtain entrance. They thought we were Turkomans, as this desolate place has a good spring of water near, which is often visited by those robbers. Rode to-day sixty-four miles.

The next morning was very sharp and cold, with hoar frost in shady places. We pushed on again, over a desolate plain covered with gravel. Did forty miles and slept at Damghan. This place is noted for the battle fought between the Afghan Shah Mahmoud's heir, Shah Ashraf, and the afterwards famous Nadir Shah, then a robber chief, in 1729, who was proclaimed Shah of Persia in 1736. (He was born 1688, and murdered near Mushud, 1747.) This is supposed to have been the ancient capital of the Parthians. Here I got my first fowl, for for the last three days I had lived on milk and bread. *Kafilas* were met going and returning from Meshed. Prince Abbas Mirza has left his mark here; for having encamped his army *en route* to besiege Herat, in 1832, the district received such a blow from the destruction caused by the thieving mob, that it has never recovered itself. Dehmullah, a wretched village, with undrinkable water, was next passed. The road leading to it was dangerous, full of open wells, even in the middle of the road; they belonged to an old dry *karize.*

Our next halt was Sharood, a small city surrounded with a mud wall, and situated in the angle between two ranges of hills, the Shavan Koh. It is a picturesque place, with large gardens of mulberries and poplars, supplied with copious streams of water that rise in the hills to the north, which are about 4000 feet high. Here I found many travellers, and the place surrounded with *zowars,* or pilgrims. The *Chappar-Khana* was full of animals, but luckily it had three rooms above, of which I secured one; the others were full of Persians. I was glad of a day's rest, so rose late; the next morning sending into the bazaar Mahomed Ali, my servant, to repair damages done to our gear, and lay in fresh supplies. I opened my small English hand-bag that contained the writing things, matches, quinine, chlorodyne, pills, tobacco, money, &c., and found that the shaking had not improved the contents, some of my precious packets of dry soup having broken, and with other things formed a thick powder at the bottom. Having carefully repacked all, and replaced the bag in the *khourjee*, or saddle bag, I took a stroll into the city.

The post-house being outside the walls, I was warned, as the city gates were shut at sunset, not to remain out late. While wandering about I came across Ali, who told me there were some Europeans here. I was so glad that I rushed off to the serai in which I heard they lived, and first found two young Armenian merchants, who kindly gave me tea, in the usual manner, and plenty of information about the silk and leather trade of the place, and spoke of another European. Thence I went off to find out their friend. He lived in another serai, and spoke a little French, but it was so rusty for want of practice that at first it was difficult to understand him, but as he warmed up he proved an interesting companion. He kindly made me stay to dinner. He was an old man, a Russian, and has been a fixture here for many years. He showed me a little native boy, an orphan, he had adopted during the famine, whom he was rearing, and said he might have purchased many such, as they were offered by the poor mothers for nothing but food. To get back to the post-house, I borrowed a pony and a lantern from the old man. The latter is absolutely necessary to light one clear of traps and pitfalls, such as dogs, mud, and sewers, which are always open and dirty in Persia. When I arrived at the city gate I found it locked, and could not get out, so I had to bribe the soldiers with a few krans to open it. Next morning went for a walk, and visited the Persian officer in command of the cavalry escort, Iskunder Bey. He received me in a tent, and was very polite, asking to see my arms, and showing me his; also informing me that, owing to the non-arrival from Teheran of a lady of high birth who was to have accompanied the harem of the Governor of Sharood on their way to Meshed, the gun escort would be delayed a few days.

I did not bless these women, as I was very anxious to push on, so asked him if I could go alone, but he laughed at the idea, as the Turkomans had been very active of late, carrying their forays up to the gates of

Bostan and Sharood, and warned me not to try, as if taken prisoner by them I might be kept a slave all my life!

After breakfast I went again o the Russian, and had another chat with the Armenians. Their serai was full of bales of cotton, wool, hides, silk, cocoons, &c., they had also a screw to press the bales with, and did a flourishing trade. While at their house I heard that the sowars had started with an escort of fifty horse. As I did not wish to lose the chance, I in a hurry had tea with Baumgarten, the Russian, while Ali got my bags ready, and arranged for our ponies; I procured a lot of old Persian coins from Baumgarten, who, as we parted, begged me not to go alone. After having taken more food at the post-house, we started with the *Chappar-Shagird*,* or post-servant, on three sorry steeds, at 7 P.M., by moonlight, and found the pilgrims at Budusht, only a few miles out, they not liking to proceed further as they had only twenty-five men for escort.

Sharood is a place of great importance, several roads meeting here, and is only about forty-five miles from

* These post-boys always accompany a traveller to bring the ponies back to their stables.

Astrabad, and seventy-five from the Caspian. From Sharood are two roads to Meshed—one, the one I went by, and the other one viâ Jahjerm Bajnurd and Kooshan, which is longer, but would be easier for a force, as water and supplies are procurable. That part of the road between Sharood and Mazeenan, a distance of about ninety-six miles, is the most dangerous for travellers, and it ought to be well protected against the Turkomans, but is not.

From Budusht I determined to push on alone, as I found it would be of no use waiting for the escort to start; and praying for the protection of the Almighty, we galloped on to the open plain in front, and after travelling all night, and nearly losing our way once, got into Meyomed at dawn. Here is one of the best and most perfect specimens of Shah Abbas's caravanserais, spacious and well-built, with a flat roof and also an avenue of shady Chinars in front. Good tobacco is grown here, as also a little silk, but the village is most miserable. They live on the little stream that gives life to this desert. The agriculture there was curious: year after year they grow tobacco in the same ground, sowing oats and barley as a second crop, and that without any manure.

Here I remained all day, and at evening started again on the same Sharood ponies, none being available here.

After another dismal night's ride, got safely into Meandhust at daylight, it being very cold. They were building a new serai there—the only place in Persia where I saw anything like a new building. In the afternoon I saw the large *kafila* of pilgrims, escorted by a few dirty *Eeljowree*, or Militia, who had charge of a wretched 4-pounder 4-horse gun, come straggling in from Abbasabad and Meshed. They asked me how I had come along, and were astonished at my venturing alone; and I asked them if they thought the Turkos would dare to attack an Englishman! At this they smiled and said, "*Inshalla*"—No. There was a small fort built on the plain at Ferashabad to keep the Turkomans in check, but the weak garrison on being threatened with an attack if they ventured to hold it again, left it and the safety of the road to its fate.

We started again in the afternoon for Abbasabad, the people of which village are said to have been the descendants of an Armenian or Georgian colony of 100 families planted by Shah Abbas. We arrived at 5 P.M., over a very bad road; a wretched place, consisting of a few fortified huts, but with a fine serai on the hill-side; a cold windy place, but being high one gets a good view of the plains of Khorasan, which is now a howling desert, all on account of Turkomans and a weak but tyrannical Government. We descended into the plain and along a dry watercourse, and after ten miles came to an old bridge in ruins, the Pul Abresham, a dangerous looking place for the man stealers, as Goklan* Yomut and Tekke often shake hands here. A serai was built here by the Sudr Azan, and therefore has been called Sudrabad. We luckily found the road free, and rode on to Mazeenan, a large ruined village, which has a good and plentiful stream of water full of small fish. This village being *yaghy*† in refusing to pay extra taxes, was depopulated a few years ago by the Government. The Subzewar district begins here, and from this a good road over a plain of red, green, and yellow gravel brought us into Mehr after sunset. This little village is watered by a muddy stream from the hills to the north; its revenue is 700 tomans; and, with the seven hamlets on the plain below, lost half its popu-

* Tribes of Turkomans which inhabit different points on the frontier.

† Rebellious.

lation in the famine. The soil is better here than the country crossed during the last two marches. They grow silk, and mulberries abounded on all sides; the stream passes down the principal street, which is shaded by Chinars. Halted for Sunday. All the roofs here, as in most parts of Persia, are domed with *Kutcha*, or sun-dried bricks, which last well in this dry climate. They are very clever in building arches and domes without any centring, the layers of bricks being self-supporting, as they are built up in a slanting direction and not vertically or horizontally. The speed with which a mud house is built is surprising, and they span as much as twenty-three feet with a *Kutcha** arch or dome. Very few of the houses are roofed with wood in Khorasan.

The old stage from Mehr to Subzewar, over a desert, used to be thirty miles long, but now they have established a *Chappar* midway at Rewayat, of which I was the first to take advantage. The approach to Subzewar is marked by extensive ruins, and by a solitary *minar*, or minaret, very strongly built, the bricks being laid in patterns with excellent taste; also the tin-

* Literally raw or uncooked. There is a great dearth of timber throughout Persia.

covered dome of an Imamzadus tomb—this is seen shining in the sun a considerable distance off. This shrine was originally covered with silver, but which has long since given place to tin. The city is large, with high bastioned walls and towers. The district round is well cultivated, but the interior of the city has a very desolate appearance.

While at the *Chappar-Khana*, amongst others who came as usual to see me was a *dervish*, singing boy. He gave us a display of his powers. The language was old Persian, which the people now hardly understand, sung out in a long drawl, on one or two keys. I soon sent him off, as he attracted too large a crowd. This is another commercial place, so I went to see the Armenian merchants. They only understood Persian, and informed me that the same description of trade goes on here as at Sharood, but not to such a large extent; amongst other things, I saw quantities of small shallow boxes of some seed, as I thought, but which proved to be silkworms' eggs, packed for importation into Georgia, and in which article they carry on a good trade.

I was surprised to find so little of the Russian element along this route. Trade was almost at a standstill, and was carried on by Armenians and French Piece-goods are mostly English. Russian goods and gold are also in use to some extent, but do not predominate, as I had expected to find them. They make here very superior felts for carpets—thick, close, and strong—termed *Koorkee.*

As I left Subzewar I met one of the governor's *gholams*, or servants, riding my road, and had a long talk with him. He said the country was badly governed, and no encouragement held out to the cultivators; but as much as possible was extorted by the local authorities, over and above the just Government dues. The road up to Zefferanee is over a flat, with a few villages on it; after that, a long stretch of wilderness, quite uninhabited It is not a sterile desert; on the contrary, the soil is good; but the cupidity of the Government and attacks of Turkomans have done their worst. After this we crossed over a spur of limestone rocks and through a pass, which had a pretty serai of brick, and good supply of water. Then we descended into a valley, partially cultivated, with a village and serai, called Shorea; which might be made a strong military position in case of an advance from Astrabad.

The ravages of the Turkomans end here, as they seldom come so far; but have attacked and sacked Nishapore, still further to the east, in times past.

The road to Nishapore is bad and stony, along the foot of a range of low, rocky hills. The country is better cultivated than usual, and we saw several villages on the plain—an unusual sight. The town is not seen from afar. The walls are old and out of repair, without any good building inside. The bazaar was very full of people, it being their weekly fair—crowded with women from adjoining villages buying cloths—and so great was the crowd, we could hardly force our way through the long, but cool, vaulted bazaar. A syrup made from the *Rewas* plant is celebrated here, and was being consumed in large quantities by the people in the shape of sherbet. This used to be a place of great importance, and watered by many *karaizes*, as it is a rich valley eighteen miles broad; and out of 800 they used to boast of, now only two or three hundred *karaizes* are in good order. The valley is very fertile, and might, with care, be made an important district again—air and water being both good. Nishapore is often mentioned in the old stories of the Bagh-o-Bahar.*

* Persian story-book.

Our next stage, Kudmgah, takes its name from an old mosque, in a garden with fine large pine trees, and an avenue of the same leading down into the plain. The village is built in a gorge of a hill, well supplied by a stream. The view of it from the east is picturesque, with its ruined forts on each side of the gorge, high upon the hills, and the green-domed mosque appearing through the trees below. This picture is set in a frame of yellow desert.

From here there are two roads to Meshed—one by Deyrood, cold and damp, by the banks of a low stream fringed by willows; and the other over the hills, a stony route. I was obliged to take the latter, as the *Chappar-Khana* is at Shareefabad, and none at Deyrood. Also a road to Turbut Sheik Hydree turns off to the south-east from here. Along this stage I met many people—large parties of women riding on donkeys, with only a few men to look after them. They, of course, wore the *boorka,* or long veil, with holes for the eyes, but were not very particular as to hiding their faces, as in the country they are allowed greater liberty. They were going on pleasure trips to Kudmgah, and would return in three or four days. In the mosque, or rather tomb, is a black stone with a slight impression on it, which the faithful believe was made by the Iman Raza's foot—Ali Raza the Eighth in descent from the Prophet—and to pray here the people were going. Men were on horses, and armed at all points. These were of a superior description to the common travellers, being young fellows, well to do, out hunting, and some riding with hawks and hounds.

All the game I saw in Persia was a flock of ravine deer, called *ahow;* also the common sand-grouse, *seeaseena,* a few partridges and larks—the grouse being plentiful round Meshed. It is a great business for the sportsmen to get off their horses and creep up as close as possible to their game, blow their matches, and fire; and not having shot, they use pebbles or ball. Powder and caps they procure from Teheran—trashy French stuff of the cheapest description, in uniformity with their arms.

The road in the hills is covered with a pretty pink quartz, which sparkles in the sun; also a green stone is common, being rough and soft like sand-stone. As it was a cold windy day I stayed at Shareefabad, which is built in a small sheltered valley. The next day's stage being a long one, the nags very bad, and the road worse, we did not arrive till dark. I felt the cold very much all night, so was up early, and started on my last *Chappar* ride of seven or eight farsaks. The road led us over hills covered with small bushes and large boulders, and being so near a large city it ought to have been in better repair. The *Sepa Salar,* or Commander-in-Chief, made a pilgrimage a few years ago, and turned one of the worst parts into a tolerably good road; but that was again fast getting into ruins. A large slab of slate, with deeply-cut inscription recording this, still stands on the roadside.

From the top of the *kotul,* or pass, called the Tuppa Salam, we obtained our first sight of the plains and hills beyond Meshed Mukudus.* My companions here stopped, and falling on their knees, said their prayers, piled a few stones together, and, trying to squeeze out a tear, made models of houses for the accommodation of themselves or friends in the future world, weeping for the martyrdom of the holy Iman Raza. Some go into fits of epilepsy by working on their imaginations. Before leaving they tore a rag off their clothes and fastened it to the nearest bush to flap in the wind.

* The Holy.

There are many villages in the valley to the north and west, but towards the east all stretches away in bare undulating plains. These villages supply fruit to the city, and in summer the people come out here to eat fruit and enjoy themselves, and here the rich have their summer-houses. It was a pleasant sight indeed to see the Holy City, with its encircling bastioned walls, and the glistening cupolas and minars of the mosques of Gohur Shad and Iman Raza. Gohur Shad was the mother of Shah Rukh Mirza, son of Tamerlane. The mosque was built by her in A.D. 1415.

How I longed for the flesh-pots of Egypt just then, uncertain with what sort of reception I should be received, as this, being a shrine, has a most fanatical and bigoted population. We passed several villages perched upon the hills, well fortified, one of which was Mooshoom. From the pass, the road down into the plain is a very bad one, and on the level ground, it is dangerous from its deep water-courses and open *karaize* wells. As we neared the city many small ruins and tombs skirted the road, with several mendicants and dervishes asking alms. We entered the city at the Eedga Gate; the ditch and walls were very dilapidated. My servant I had sent on to clean out a room in the *Chappar-Khana*, so the post-boy, or *shagird*, and I were alone. On entering, they asked me to pay the usual tax, and to show the contents of my saddle-bags. Of course I refused to do this, as Europeans are exempt from all such payments. Then they caught hold of the boy's horse and detained him; but I told them to open the bags at their peril, and rode on. As I was asking my way a man called out, "Catch hold of his horse; he hasn't paid toll." They did so, saying I must go back and pay. But I said, "If you must look into my bags, come to the post-house and see;" and striking the rascal holding my horse across the back with my *kamcheen*, or whip, I left him bellowing on the ground. After this they did not molest me, as it is a well-understood thing in Persia that no European or rich native is put to the indignity of having his effects searched in public. After a long search I found the *Chappar-Khana*—right glad to have got over so much of my journey. Distance: 149 farsaks, or about 580 miles.

MESHED TO HERAT.

The Governor of Khorassan—My Dress and Equipment—State Visit—Executed Turkomans—The Holy of Holies—Hummum, "Our" Native Agent—Preparations—Escort Departure—About Merv—Horse Training—Rahdaree—Turbut—Force at Tybat—Frontier of Persia—Approach to Herat—My Reception.

I SENT off my letter to our Vakeel, Mirza Abbas Khan, early next morning, not having passed a good night, as an attack of fever and ague had kept me awake till near morning. At 8 A.M. the Vakeel came to see me, and, like a good man as he was, brought a horse for me to ride, as he insisted on my going to stay with him. Our route lay along the Kheeaba, or principal street of the city, crowded at that hour with a motley stream of men and animals; and as a canal runs down the centre and has trees on each side, this street is a favourite place of resort. We saw many men mounted, and leading their long strings of horses with great heavy *numda* coverings; *kafilas* of donkeys, with pinewood and *kah* or *bhoosa*,* and camels with merchandise, profusions of grapes and

---

* Straw chaff.

melons, vegetables of all sorts, and the usual sights of a crowded Eastern bazaar. When we came near the great mosque, we dived down a small street to the right, which was arched over—above being the houses of some Bey. At the end of this dark tunnel was a door that led us into the outer court of the Vakeel's house. Having dismounted, he gave me the usual greeting as I passed his threshold—"*Bismillah!*"*—and conducted me to an upper room, with coloured glass windows on all sides, called *Oorsee*, overlooking his garden, beyond which was his *Zenan-khana*. "*Bismillah khush amadeed!*" ("You are welcome!") was the signal for us to sit down, and in came the tea and *kullyan*, and with it lots of people to see me—or *Hal Pursee*, as they term it, which means, to ask after your health—and hear the latest Teheran news (as I had beaten the *cossid*, who did not arrive till the day after). When at last they had taken their leave, only one man remained. He proved to be a pensioned Ressaldar of our Bengal Cavalry, here on some Government duty from India. He gave me much information, and proved useful during my stay. The Vakeel then

* "In the name of God."

went to the Governor of Khorasan, the Hisame Sultunut Prince Moorad Mirza, the Sword of the State, fifth son of Prince Abbas Mirza, son of the former Shah-in-Shah, Futteh Ali Shah. This personage is, after his relative the Shah, the most powerful in the kingdom, about fifty years of age; has the reputation of being a soldier, and is tolerably just for a Persian. He is a man of great energy and influence, consequently the Shah is jealous of him. He has been Governor of Khorasan since 1850, shortly after he took Meshed from the insurgents who rose in rebellion at the last king's, Mahomed Shah, death. I hoped to get some help from him in the way of an escort to Herat, also a letter to Mahomed Yakoob Khan. All assured me I should have no difficulty in going there.

I had to purchase horses and ponies, and set myself up with a servant and a few provisions, &c., as across this country there were no caravanserais or *Chappar* horses. In the evening I had another fit of ague—I am afraid from eating too much fruit, which is delicious here.

The report here about the Seistan Commission was that Generals Goldsmid and Pollock could do next to nothing, being afraid of surveying even, so hostile were the people; even food was refused their followers, so they had to leave after four days' unsuccessful negotiation.

On the second day I began to get my native dress ready, and had in a lot of the Vakeel's friends to give advice as to the proper cut of *shalwars,* or baggy-trousers, large enough to have taken in a baby on each side; also as to the style and pattern of the embroidery of my *sirdaree,* or greatcoat, double-breasted, with a high collar; also waistcoat, *kulla-loongee,* the cap and turban, sword-belt, and *shum-sher,* or sword, of true Persian shape. When these things were ready, on the fourth day I went out swaggering as good as the best of them. I also bought a fine Turkomanee horse, with gaudy trappings; also two ponies, with their *palans,* or pack-saddles: so that on the fifth day I was ready to start. I went for several rides, when trying horses, not only along the Kheeaba, but outside the walls and neighbouring villages. *Zowars,* or pilgrims, from all parts of Persia come here in numbers—about 20,000 to 30,000 yearly—and many bring the bones of their dead relatives to be buried here. One meets many green-and-white turbaned Syeds and Moollahs in the streets, all on the look-out for their prey—the poor pilgrims to whom they teach, for a consideration, the proper ceremonies of their pilgrimage. The city is full of graveyards, which are crammed with graves, but within the last few years orders have been given not to bury any more inside the walls; so great, however, is the desire of all that die here to be buried within the shade of the Holy City, that they often bury by stealth. Cholera and dysentery are common enough, with a change to small-pox when the city gets too full. No one thinks of death, though they ever live in the midst of it.

In the afternoon of the third day I went by appointment to visit the Prince at his residence in the Ark, or citadel, the approach to which does not give one any idea of its strength, nor, indeed, has it any real strength. The place is spacious enough. We were led through many passages and courts, at last coming to one of large size, with high walls and a garden in the centre, with large water-tanks full of fish. At the end we were led up some steps to the *Balakhana*, an oblong room looking out into the garden. It was nicely carpeted, and had two iron camp chairs, its only furniture. After a moment's delay the Governor came in with a few of his *pesh-kidmuts* and *Nazir*—a small man, rather fair, dressed in European-cut trousers and frogged military frock-coat; it being cold, he had on a fur-lined *choga* of brown cloth. I had my undress uniform on, and was not required to take my boots off. I took off my cap on his entering, but he begged me to put it on, as I might catch cold! After asking about my journey (of which he seemed to know all particulars), and as to how I dared to venture alone through the dangerous districts, he wished to know if I had been in the Abyssinian campaign, saying they thought it wonderful we had left the country after conquering it, our disposition for annexing being evidently on his mind. Then he asked after the Governor-General and Commander-in-Chief, Lord Napier of Magdala, and gave me advice about the route to Herat, saying he was going to give me an escort of forty horsemen, with an introductory letter to Yakoob Khan, for which I thanked him. He then got up and led me into the garden, and showed me some specimens of marble he had had dug out of the hills to the west of the city, also some rather well-made *teapoys*, or tables, of the same, that he was going to send as presents to Teheran.

On leaving him I went to see the guns, which were parked in the square in front. They were old ones of all sorts—six-pounder, nine-pounder, and twelve-pounder—Russian, French, and English, with rotten carriages that would not have stood any very hard work. He has about thirty guns of all sorts, some only two and three-pounders. The soldiers were a slovenly lot, worse than at Teheran, with badly-kept arms.

While on the way home I saw a dreadful sight. On a dead wall, at the end of a lane, were three men crucified; they had large wooden tent-pegs driven through the hands and feet, and one through the back, with their faces to the wall. It made me shudder; one glance being sufficient. These unfortunates were three Turkomans the Governor had lately caught red-handed in a raid on some village in the neighbourhood. These wretches are the terror of the country, and richly deserved death, but not such a dreadful one; for, to prolong the torture, the peg through the back was left in: had it been extracted they would have died at once. Some caught before had been flayed alive, and left to die by inches.

They told me that eighty chiefs of the Turkomans had been invited to a conference at Meshed, and had been treacherously seized. So much for the civilisation of Persia! This was by the order of one of the most accomplished men of his time.

Passing up the Kheeaba homewards, we had to pass by the tomb of Imam Raza; and though escorted by the Prince's servants, I was advised not to go in, though I longed to go close and inspect its beautifully decorated front of glazed tiles, and to ascend its gilt minars.

The square in which all the holy buildings are situated is called the Sahn. As this has been so well described before, I will only give my first impressions of this Sahn, as far as I could see from outside, and what I was told. The Kheeaba, that runs in a straight line from gate to gate right through the city, is divided into two parts by this square. The entrance into this square is through high-arched gates, of graceful architecture, faced with blue-glazed tiles. After entering, you see on all sides a double-storied row of arched cloisters, faced with different coloured marbles; and the square is paved with large slabs of marble and sandstone, which on close inspection prove to be tombstones. The privilege of being allowed to be buried in the sacred enclosure is only granted to those of high rank, who can afford to pay heavily. From the square, leading into smaller squares, are five arched gateways, such as are on the Kheeaba. one leads into a mosque, and is covered with blue tiles; another leads into the square of the tomb of Imam Raza, and is covered with copper gilt tiles. The dome of the tomb and the minarets on each side are all beautifully gilt, and shew in the far distance glittering in the sun. In the centre of the Sahn is a small temple, with a reservoir for water for the ablutions of the faithful. The square round the tomb itself is a sanctuary, to which malefactors flee and find a safe refuge; a few houses of Moollahs also are in it, and a few shops for the sale of various small beads and *souvenirs* of this Holy of Holies of the Sheahs. All is in such beautiful proportion, and so profusely decorated, that few buildings can compare with it, although Meshed was sacked by the Uzbegs in 1587; but the great Shah Abbas rebuilt it in 1595, and they say, that these buildings are as they were first built.

On the fourth evening I told the Vakeel that I

had a great wish to have a hot bath, or hummum. This, he said, was rather difficult to obtain, but he would try; so he sent off one of his servants to bribe a hummumjee to let me in after the day's work was over, and his clients had left. In this he succeeded for the sum of ten krans; so after dark, when the streets were left to the dogs—who then get very savage—the Mirza and I, in long *chogas*, or cloaks, with a lantern in front and a man to keep off the dogs, sneaked along the dirty, narrow lane, and were quietly admitted into a bath-house, and the door strongly barred after us. The inside was octagonal, with a lofty dome, borne on square pillars, with a raised dais all round, in the centre being a well of cold water. Here, undressing, we were clothed with towels of blue and yellow check, and led off to the "hot" room, a large domed, flag-floored place, with a hot flue passing underneath, one side of which was the hot bath itself. Into this we jumped to keep ourselves warm, while the bathing-man was getting ready to torture us. I first had half an hour's dreadful bruising and shampooing; then the Mirza got his share. Returning to dress in the "cold" room, which had been lit up during our absence, we were served with coffee and *kulyoons* while drying and resting. The roof was covered with huge coloured pictures of Persian heroes, such as Rustum and Nowsherwan, Yousuf and Zuleika, and others; also tigers catching antelope, &c. This was a woman's bath, and they would have been in a great rage if they knew that a *Kafir** had been polluting it by his presence. We got back safe, however, feeling wonderfully well after it all. Next day being my last, I had plenty to do—laying in provisions of tea, sugar, rice, butter, &c.; also warm gloves, and long, wool-lined riding-boots, such as the natives wear.

My friend gave me one of his own servants, Hadjee Mahomed Khan, to accompany me as far as Candahar, of which he was a native. This man also went as servant to Herat with Colonel Taylor in 1858—the last European who had been there before me. The Vakeel, Abbas Khan, is a Government pensioner, his family having done us good service at Candahar during the Cabul campaign. After our leaving that country all his father's property was confiscated by the Amir, so he is now quite dependent on us. He gets twelve

* Unbeliever.

tomans pension, with twenty five more as pay from the British Legation at Teheran; total, thirty-seven tomans per mensum—not near enough to keep up his position and influence in the city: it ought to be at least fifty.*

At the last moment came a message from the Prince, saying that the Turkomans were out and the road unsafe These might have been some of the Turbut-i-Hydree people, who also get up *Alamans* when they think they can do so with impunity, as they are regular highway robbers. But as I had determined to start the next day, I sent word that if he wished to honour me with an escort it must be ready at the Herat Gate by sunrise, or else I should start without it. Next morning I was up betimes, but found that the household was not. During the cold weather the Persians do not rise early (except the poor, who have to go to their work), spending the evening, and far into the night, in eating, drinking, and often using freely spirituous liquors, relating tales, and singing to the music of a description of

* Estimating the kran at 6 annas, this would only amount to Rs. 186½, or about £18.

guitar. They were disinclined to rise as early as I wished them to do on that morning. In their social meetings women, of course, are carefully excluded from the society of their lords, and have to enjoy themselves in the seclusion of their apartments; even among most intimate friends, man and woman are always apart. Finding I could not rouse the people, I began taking my traps down into the court-yard and looking to the stuffing of the pack-saddles, as on the fitness of these would depend my powers of progression; all *palans* or pack-saddles being made on the same plan, it only remains to fit them to the backs of the ponies for whom they may be destined. This is done by means of slips of *numda*, or felt, being tacked on inside, so as to take the weight off the withers and backbone, throwing it on the ribs. A traveller must be very careful on this point, as Persian servants are of a very cruel and careless disposition, paying little heed to the comfort of the pack-yaboos* under their charge. As I had two ponies, they were not heavily laden, only having to carry their nose-bags and the horse's heavy *numdas* and ropes in addition to their

* Ponies.

own, with the man perched on the top of all. At the last moment I was glad to hear a rattle at the outer gate, which awoke the people, and on opening it in came a lot of wild-looking men, armed and booted for the road, bringing several letters from the Prince to the different places on the way I should pass. They reported themselves quite ready to start, and their leader, a young Turkoman, himself in the service of the Shah, added, "To protect your honour against the faithless thieves"—regardless of his relationship to them, and as ready to cut their throats as they would certainly be if they caught hold of his. Giving the Resseldar, Daood Khan, who had been so useful to me, and his companion, Ramzan Ali Khan, notes of recommendation, and putting a few gold coins into the hands of the Vakeel's little daughter, in exchange for his expense in keeping me, we started.

As my cavalcade debouched out of the narrow streets into the Kheeaba, it must have been about 9 A.M.; but I am not certain, as I left my watch, rings, &c., all at home before starting for Constantinople, so as not to excite the cupidity of any one. We made a fine show, clearing the road for the

"*Elchi Sahib*,"* as they called me. We went out by the Herat Gate, and then my friends, who had come so far to do me honour, left me with many "*Khush Bashed*" and "*Khuda Hafiz*." After proceeding a short distance to clear the gardens and walls in the immediate vicinity of the city, I halted to look back on the last link that tied me to Europe. After this I should be left entirely to my own devices, and under the protection of the Almighty Power, in whom was my only hope. My companions were wild brutes in the guise of men, who would have been glad to see me taken off by the first *Alaman*. Mounted on all sorts of animals, and armed in any way they pleased, I had little trust in the "escort" the Prince had honoured me with. I forgot to mention that the Prince's Lord Chamberlain, or *Mutawllee Bashee*, is his uncle, Saifudowla, son of Futteh Ali Shah, a venerable old man of seventy, said not to be nearly so liberal-minded as his nephew the Governor, objecting to Europeans being allowed to visit the holy city, Meshed.

* Somehow, when leaving Teheran, my first servant, Ali, would have it I was an "ambassador" from Constantinople going to Kashgar with secret despatches—so the name.

The first march is to Sungbust,* an old village and caravanserai, walled, of course, which used to be the residence of a colony of Afghans, under Sirdar Mahomed Yusoof Khan Sudozaie, who used to be the curse of traders and travellers thirty years ago. Now it is in ruins, and in it I passed a tolerable night. Early next day I was surprised by the chief of my escort asking for his dismissal, saying I should have another set of men to take me on further, thus changing my escort daily. I gave him a toman and let him go, seeing it was useless urging him to go further; and now I saw the hollowness of the arrangement. This village is supposed to furnish one hundred mounted men by way of militia, instead of being taxed. A few of these were sent on with me. To beguile the monotony of the march I made it a rule to inquire from the most intelligent of my surroundings for any information the country afforded. One of these men had just returned from a journey to Merv or Mawar, the chief camp of the Turkomans. This place, since it was destroyed by Nadir Shah, in 1741, and after that by the Amir of

* This was V. Baker's furthest in October, 1873. He makes a slight allusion to me. Abbas Khan accompaneid him on his travels.

Bokhara, Begi Jan, in 1787, had never been rebuilt; and to this day, though called the chief town of the Turkomans, does not contain a single house. At certain seasons of the year, after harvest, the tribes assemble here with the produce of farm or flock, and pitch their black goats' hair or felt tents amid the ruins of the ancient Shah Jehan. The nearest tribes are the Tekke, Sarik, Salor, and Kara Turkomans, the former being the most powerful and the greatest scourge of the Sheeahs. In the great heats the town is again deserted, the River Murgab being then nearly, and often quite, dry. A Persian army was destroyed by the Turkomans in 1860, while attempting to seize Merv, which shows how bad the Persian troops are.

The whole march to Furriman is devoid of water; the country is easy to traverse, but quite deserted. This village is a military fief of an hundred sowars* to Meshed; it has lots of good land round it, but lacks water and security from plunder. With these, being situated in a narrow valley, it might easily be made into a strong bar to the road to Herat. Though there are several parallel roads, both north and south,

* Mounted men.

this valley is the only one where water is certain to be found, and is, moreover, the nearest in point of distance, about forty-five miles from Meshed. Next day I went off with only four sowars, the Mulik,* Abdoolla Khan, saying that all his men had gone with his son to join a force which was forming to intercept a large Salor Alaman that had penetrated along the Persian-Herat frontier. At a couple of farsaks further is Kullunderabad, a village which has lately been plundered and ruined; and by some trees near a spring I found a lot of Persians collected; as I neared them two well-mounted young fellows dashed out and saluted me; one of them was the son alluded to, Hussan Khan, twenty-five years of age. He told me he had heard of my arrival, and wished to accompany me to the frontier. The road was bad and stony, with small hills on both sides, from behind one of which a party of Turkos had looted a caravan a few weeks before. He wanted me to go on to Abdullabad, but as I heard that Burdoo was a better place, we passed the night together there. He said that the Persian army was not properly paid, but that the men were really of good stuff if well led. The country wanted fostering. No large force could pass along this route but with previous arrangements, as the supplies would fail, the few villages only producing just enough for themselves. The people were very quiet, and ready to obey any one who protected them. On Monday I was glad to get away from this place, Burdoo, my quarters during Sunday having been a stable! This day I had only one man as guide, all the rest were away with the force.

At Abdullabad, a few miles off, I found a nice little village, famous for its fruit gardens, and well watered by a small stream from the *karez* on the hill to the south. It also used to produce silk. The country here becomes open again, flat, with undulations, a good road, but rather roundabout; the path direct between Burdoo and Mahmoodabad would only have been three farsaks instead of five. The latter village is seen afar off; it has good water, standing on high ground over the stream that comes from Abdullabad. Here I saw rich green fields, crops of barley and wheat, just cut, also lucern grass for winter fodder. The use of this plant is universal, in this dry country grass is scarce, the horses being fed on straw chaff, or *kah*, like bullocks in India, mixed with lucern, which is called severally *aluf*, *buda*, *sibbis*, and *unja*. This, with dry *jow*, *oorbush*, or barley, is their only food, and where I could get it plentifully I used to give lucern only. The usual allowance per horse is two *mun kah*, one *mun buda*, one *mun jow* = twenty-four pounds per diem. A Persian *mun* is about six pounds. In front of Mahmoodabad is the ruin of the ancient city of Linger; the only ruin I saw was an *abambar*, or reservoir of water, and a tomb, both *pukka**—the latter said to be of an Imam, a relative to Imam Raza of Meshed. This, they say, accounts for the fertility of the soil, producing wheat once, and barley twice, a year. The village is an estate belonging to the Prince Murad Mirza; and his *kaimmokam*, or manager, is Hussan Khan, a disagreeable surly fellow, who would not be hospitable to me till I showed him his master's firman, at which he and his men grovelled, so I sent them all out, calling them inhospitable dogs. All over the East travellers of the better class go in at once, without invitation, into the court, and ask for the *mehmankhanah*, or guest-house. This affords you shelter at least (I had no tents); and if the host be a good fellow he is sure to feed you, as

* Burnt brick.

well as your animals; if not, food can always be bought. This churl told me there was no guest-house, but gave me a small peasant's hut—quite new, however—instead. The following is the translation of the *rakdaree*, or firman, I got from the Prince:—

"To the exalted, eminent, and renowned chiefs of Jami:—Be it known that, stage by stage, with every care, on the route between Meshed the Holy and Karez, accompany the exalted, praised, and the well-favoured by God, Captain Marsh, Sahib, of the English service, a resident of Lahore. Foster him with every care; he is proceeding, march by march, at his convenience to Herat. From the place of his departure I am sending sowars with him, that they may guard him to Sungbust, and the sowars of Sungbust take him to Kullunderabad, and the sowars of Kullunderabad guide him to Furriman; in like manner, sowars from each stage must be sent with him till he arrives at Karez, and a messenger be sent on to Kohsan, that Kohsani sowars may conduct him safely onwards. The lofty one mentioned in this, you will treat with the greatest respect, with care and assiduity of arrangement, conduct him march by march at his ease and pleasure, and for our sake conduct him without delay; and when the Sahib reaches Karez, and the

Kohsani sowars have arrived, send them with him, and take a receipt for his safe delivery at the frontier, and also at Kohsan.

"(Seal of HUSSANI SULTANAT.)"

From here the whole country onwards to Herat is dry and hot At the last camp I had left behind some *numdas* by mistake, and to-day I was glad to find that the chief had sent them on to me. I got away with pleasure from Mahmoodabad, with only one old man as guide; he came halfway, and then, pointing to a distant hill which was our direction, said he must go back; and being useless, I let him go. The country was becoming more open, the hills on each side receding, leaving a rolling open plain; no villages *en route*, but a few ruined forts visible, showing that the country used to be more populous. The stream from Abdullabad was still running parallel with us; but down in the centre of the valley, half a mile off the road, the water all going to waste. The people I met on the road were changing; the Persian costume giving place to the *lungee* and *choga*; the *kulla*, or sheepskin hat, is becoming short and round-topped, instead of tall and square. My halting-place for to-day is the important village of Turbut-i-Skeikh Jam, from which the tribe takes its name, and here it was that the Governor of Khorasan halted his army for some time previous to the last siege of Herat by the Persians in 1856. Sheikh Jami was a poet who died three hundred years ago; his tomb (*turbut*) is a place of pilgrimage, and much venerated; he flourished at the court of Hussain Mirza, the Timuridi king of Khorasan. Some dispute this, saying it was founded long before the poet's birth by a Sheikh Jam.

Here, while drinking at a stream, my horse got away and galloped off to the village, leaving me to walk the last mile. Young Hussan Khan, of Furriman, came out to meet me, leading my horse, and hoping I had not been thrown; he, having gone off yesterday in a great hurry, had preceded me here, and now conducted me into his father-in-law's castle, where I had very good quarters over the gateway that led into the "ark," or keep, and overlooked the bazaar. The place is surrounded with walled gardens, and produces silk, fruit, and the ordinary crops.

Turbut was looted by Alla Kouli Khan, Khan of Khiva, in 1825, who overran the whole country, taking off as prisoners and slaves the population of entire villages. This *Alamanee chappau* was a daring feat, and caused the destruction of the surrounding district, no one daring to return to such a dangerous neighbourhood; and it is only lately it has begun to recover itself. The horses are specially trained for the *Alamans* on little food and less water for a month previous to an expedition; and when they once start the horse gets large quantities of a mixture of one-half barley, one quarter maize, and one quarter sheeps' fat, all made into a soft mass of eight pounds, on which the horse is able to do his hundred miles a day for several days.

Wednesday morning saw me off at daybreak, as the march is a very long one. Hussan Khan I left asleep, last night's feast having been too much for him. The country here is very nearly flat; though the soil is good, it is a wilderness—thirty-six miles without a tree or habitation. I saw large herds of antelope in the distance, which greatly frightened my servant; their dust he made out into an *Alaman.* All by ourselves in this desert, we were at the mercy of any marauders; and while resting at noon by the conical ruin of a water-tank—as all these wayside tanks to catch rain-water are always domed—we saw a lot of horsemen following our route, but were glad when they turned out to be Hussan Khan and his men. He seemed rather ashamed at being so late, saying he had stayed up late last evening writing to the heads of different villages to send their young men to join in the attack!! We went on together as far as Karez, a small fortified village, on the frontier of Persia and Herat. Here we had news that there was no one in the village to entertain me, as all the men had gone to Tybut to join the force after the Turkos; but as I was too tired to go any further, I got a shake-down in the miserable little room in the basement of one of the corner towers, and it was late before I had my dinner and fell asleep. Hussan Khan went on to Tybut, six miles further.

Now I did not want to go to Tybut, a small fort on the frontier, as it was out of my road to Kohsan, but was obliged to do so, as the Persian officers in command of the frontier, with all the people, were gathered together there, and it was with difficulty I found a man to show me the way. He told me I should see a large force encamped there. The road ran over a series of small sandy hills, and we passed a few huts. Beyond these hills lies a valley; and the chain of higher hills called Dukhter Sung, to the east, that marks a part of the frontier, rose beyond the valley. From the last hill, before reaching the fort, I got a good view of the army assembled. The few white tents were for the chiefs; the sowars had their horses picketed about in great confusion, each taking up a position as he chose. From the distance the whole did not seem to number above two or three hundred, which, when I arrived, I found to be correct. This is what they called an army, and was collected from all parts of the country round!

My friend Hussan had made things smooth for me, so I had a room given me in the fort next door to the Commandant, a Persian Sirdar, Abdool Baghee Khan, a Candaharee. He has been long in the Kajar's service, and was sent from Meshed to look after the frontier as soon as the Seistan boundary question came to the front. The fort is curiously built. As soon as you enter, all the side streets have houses over them, the road going under the houses; and it is at first quite dark, with little head room for mounted men. After several turnings I found myself in a narrow court, with stairs leading up to the rooms above; and, dismounting, I was led into the Sirdar's presence. He was just up, he said, after a bad night. We had a long talk over the hopes of capturing the *Alaman* on its return. It was reported to have advanced as far as Kaff, a town many miles to the south-west. During our conversation that day he asked for medicine, of course, and also as to what firearms I had with me, if I was married, &c.; in fact, taking stock of me generally. Amongst my traps I had a Persian Testament, which I showed him. Taking it into his hands, he kissed it, put it to his forehead with great reverence, and began reading. After getting through a few lines, he said it was a very good book, that they also reverenced the *Bebee Miriam* (Virgin Mary) and *Isa Shereef* (Jesus Christ), and then began telling me his version of Bible history, wishing to try and get up an argument, out of which I luckily escaped. Then he whispered into my ear, "Would you like some wine? We'll drink together, as there is no one here." But at this moment some people came in to see me, to his great disgust. This is the usual character of these Persians—one moment religious, another frivolous; just as the vane of a weathercock, they turn at a moment's notice, as their fickle passions move them.

Tybut, being such an obscure place, is generally deserted, the Sirdar's head-quarters being Karez. So the *Alaman* had taken the opportunity to go past that fort in the night, and its track was only marked by the smoke of the burning villages it had destroyed on its way inland. This occurred ten days ago; so now he hoped to catch some of the Turkos on their return. The whole of this part of the country is depopulated right up to the banks of the Hurri Rood, and belongs to—or rather is occupied by—no one, being left as a high road for the Turkoman depredators. Such is the culpable inertness of both Persian and Afghan Governments. A small force posted at Kaffir Killa, an old ruined fort in the centre of the *Alamanee* track, well disciplined and armed, would soon put a stop to the vile man-hunters—in this part, at least.

At first, next day, the Sirdar refused to give me any escort, saying he wanted all the men he had; but after my threatening to report him at Meshed, he consented to my taking a mounted man to show me the road. Fortunately, I found a few people outside the encampment, who were anxiously waiting for me, hoping to cross the dangerous frontier in my company. On my arrival here yesterday the Sirdar had sent off my papers for Yakoob Khan, and a letter to the Afghan officer in command of their frontier post of Koshan, asking him to send some sowars to Kafir Killa to take charge of me. This place was entirely ruined since the last Persian siege of Herat by Nussaroddeen, in October, 1856. But the ruin began in 1818, in the wars between Persia, under Mahomed Shah, and the Afghans. The road was a very easy one, over a sandy rolling country. We were about twenty altogether, including three women, riding behind some of the men. The party was badly armed, being only traders, who had sold goods at Karez, and had long been on tne look-out for an opportunity of going back to Herat. As we left our only protection behind, and launched forth over the inhospitable plain, the prayers uttered were not a few, mingled with sundry *Inshallas*, for our safe arrival. We had many false alarms from clouds of dust, and in several places saw the recent tracks of the robbers' horses. When we got to Kafir Killa the Persian sowar asked for my writing, or receipt, saying he had taken me safely over the border.

I found no Afghans awaiting me, as none had been sent, because the officer, Julleel Khan, was at Herat. So, again trusting to Providence, I let the *Iranee* go, and gave him a paper. I took this opportunity of also sending a line to my Teheran friends. This place has a small tank of water, which is used by the Turkomans as a resting-place. Our greatest danger was when we arrived on the banks of the Hurri Rood, which is thickly wooded—in fact, a regular jungle. In this we hoped not to find our slavery or death. The river had very little water at this season, it being exhausted by the canals, taken off at the different villages higher up. The stream itself is only two yards wide, and a foot deep, but the bed is more than 1000 yards broad, with islands and also deep pools in various parts, and full of tall grass and prickly bushes. The natives say it is seldom full. Having crossed over, we found fresh fires and tracks of the Turkomans. They must have fled, thinking us a strong body. From hence on to Kohsan is two farsaks, which we soon traversed. This Afghan frontier fort used to be populated once, but now a dilapidated wall and a few huts and walled gardens are all that remain. I stayed here for the night, being entertained by the Naib, and had to eat with some half-dozen dirty Afghans out of the same dish. After dinner we got *khubber** that an *Alaman* had taken off a flock of 600 sheep, and off he had to go after them;—such, he said, was his usual occupation. While such insecurity occurs, how can they expect to see the country cultivated? Kohsan is said to have been a large fort and town, and to have withstood a long siege by Jenghis Khan. It had been forsaken

---

* News.

in 1827 by its inhabitants because of the increasing attacks of the Turkomans, and it is only within the last ten years that it has begun to show signs of life, such life as it is, only in its defensive form—miserably small fields enclosed by walls, all the approaches to the village being between these high walls; one sees in front of one at every turn the loopholed wall opposite.

During the night we had torrents of rain, and when we started next morning it was still pouring hard. The wet bags and *numdas* were a heavy load for the poor Yaboos, so we went along slowly, accompanied by some Turkoman horse-dealers, who had arrived from Merv during the night, and had disturbed my slumbers. They had a few horses for sale, but as they only spoke Turkee, they could not converse with me in Persian. The country is hilly and quite desolate; road easy, running parallel to the river, which can be traced by its densely-wooded banks. My next stage was a short one, to Subush; a little, mean, dirty fort, hardly habitable. Shortly after my arrival here, Abdool Zahir Khan, Governor of Ghorian, a fort of some strength, with Julleel Khan, and Sirdar Mahomed Yakoob Khan's servant, Shere Mahomed Khan, together with some sowars, came to conduct and welcome me to Herat.

Monday, 18*th.*—Started late, owing to rain. The Sirdars and sowars accompanied me, being ordered to do so by Yakoob Khan; and a most agreeable company they were. The road goes along the high grounds at some distance from the river; gravel soil, and a vast plain with distant hills on both sides. We passed the fort of Rozanak, and saw Ghorian in the distance, a large village, about a farsak off, on the left bank of the river: the revenue of this village is 6000 tomans, and it supports 400 sowars, as militia, who hold "free" lands, or *Teool*, on condition of military service. At Rozanak we stopped to see some curiously-made windmills, erected on the bastions of the village. The windy season, they say, lasts about four months, and blows from the north, and comes regularly; so windmills are more common here than water-mills. They worked horizontally, and had six arms, on which were hung mats as sails. They were not in motion when I passed, and I have never seen another example of a mill of this description in any part of Asia. An old Shah Abba's caravanserai in ruins was passed; then over a bad water-covered road, being a network of canals from the river, to Shakhewan, a large group of three villages and forts, where we rested for the night. Herat, they say, was last year nearly ruined by famine, but Yakoob Khan gave quantities of grain and many bullocks to the peasants, and rescued them from destruction. The Hurri Rood has a dam thrown across it above the city, from which many canals are conducted, which water the whole plain, and one of them enters the city.

Tuesday, 19*th*.—Started off with my large retinue, which is daily increasing, taking the higher road under the hills to the left, to avoid the wet cultivation near the river; so that we went out of our way two farsaks. We begin now to enter the Joolgha, or plain of Herat, a sandy loam which bears good crops by irrigation. The country being rather flat, canals from the river have to be made many miles up, so as to get sufficient fall. Passed a lot of large villages far off to the right. These proved to be Ghorian. Here Abdul Zahir Khan begged of me to come and honour his castle for the night; but as I was anxious to reach Herat, I refused to go then, but offered to come and see him if he liked afterwards. His was a true native's answer: "That is impossible. You would not be able to see my 'lamp' after the 'sun' of Herat."

Four high minars show the site of Herat far off; and we passed large herds of camels* grazing, also flocks of sheep and goats. About two miles from the city, Sirdar Atta Mahomed Khan, Shaghasee, or Chamberlain, and others of Yakoob Khan's officers met me, with a cloud of sowars well-mounted and armed. They intended it as a great honour, and conducted me into the city between the two old minars I had seen in the distance, through the Durwaz Mulik, to my abode near the Charbagh, where the Sirdar Yakoob Khan lives. That gateway was the scene of Pottinger's great feat during the Persian siege of Herat, in June 1838, which lasted from November 1837 to September 1838. I was mobbed on all sides with salutations, and at last was glad to eat in peace the plentiful dinner sent me, after which I enjoyed a hummum and a good night's rest.

Herat, in 1716, was seized by the Sudozaie tribe of Duranees, and they held it till taken from them by Nadir Shah after a long siege in 1731. Of its history more anon.

* Here seen very nearly in a state of Nature, as they are permitted to breed while roaming free as air. The only spot where the camel is now found wild is on the vast deserts west of the great Lake Lob, in Eastern Turkestan, and of which little is known.

HERAT AND YAKOOB KHAN.

My First Audience—A Bird's-eye View of the City—An Afghan Meal—The Fort—History of his Adventures—Mosque of Mosulla—Adieu *Alamans*—Herat Army—Remarks on Policy.

THE apartments that Yakoob Khan had prepared for me, and called Khane Mushko Khan, were close to the Charbagh, his own residence. They consisted of a suite of three rooms, all looking out into a small enclosed garden, and attached to this was a hummum and dressing-room. The principal rooms were whitewashed with a mixture of pounded mica and lime, which, when the lights were lit, gave a pretty sparkle to the walls. The ceiling and floor were covered with nice new white sheeting, and everything was very clean. My animals were picketed in a corner of the garden, and outside the gate was an Afghan guard to keep out all intruders. Three servants were told off to attend to my wants, and the Sirdar deputed his favourite servant, Shere Mahomed Khan, to sit and talk with me.

In the early morning I found the horses' *jhules*, or blankets, covered with hoar-frost, as also the ground.* About 10 A.M. they brought me word that the Sirdar Sahib would like to see me when it was most convenient to myself. So then and there, putting on my uniform, the only European clothing I had, I sent to say I would see him in half an hour. A fine Heratee horse, with an English saddle and bridle, was sent for my *sowaree*, and twenty officers, &c., to escort me through the town. Although the distance was only two hundred yards, I had to go slowly to get through the narrow winding streets, full of spectators. Each housetop and point of vantage was occupied, to see the Feringhee, or stranger. The Charbagh is an enclosed palace in the centre of the town, and has nothing to boast of, being mostly built of mud. The *Arz*, or audience-hall, is of brick, as also an apartment opposite in which the Shahghasee and a few other officers live. The square in which these apartments are situated is about fifty yards square, with a tank of water in the centre. There are no trees or garden here, all being gravelled, and looking like a private

* Winter sets in early, and lasts for four months, when snow covers the hills and ice binds up all the streams.

parade-ground, where the chief's eye might organise an expedition or army without the knowledge of the townspeople or strangers.

On my being introduced to Yakoob Khan by the officers who had come with me from the frontier, he rose and met me half-way, shaking hands in European fashion. Having seated me on the small but rich carpet that formed his *musnud*, he sat close on my right, near the window that looked out on the large square. The rest of the room was filled by chiefs and officers of his army. He was dressed in a European military braided blue coat, with black trousers, socks, the Heratee sheepskin *kulld,* or hat, and a fine cloth *choga;* and his gold-belted sword lay in front at his feet. He is twenty-six years old; well-bred; has a pleasant, intelligent face; not very fair; middle height (five feet three inches); small hands and feet; slight moustache, with a slightly retreating forehead; good voice. Shaghasee Atta Mahomed Khan is a tall man; looks like a Persian, but is not so, and has lost a front tooth, which disfigures an otherwise handsome face: he is nephew to Sheredil Khan, the Shaghasee at Cabul. Sirdar Mahomed Hussun Khan, the Vizier, is a fair, round-faced, stout young man, also there was Gholam Jan, but I forget him. General Eukeer Ahmed Khan, commanding the forces, is a Cabulee Rika, thirty years old, and was with Yakoob Khan when he last took Herat. The above three or four men are generally with him, together with a few chiefs from the district, who come to pay their respects. In the centre of the room was the usual brazier of live charcoal placed on a wooden tray, which was again on a small round red felt, around which sat, in Persian Court fashion, all the audience, very respectful in their manner to their young chief. As I looked round the assembly, none seemed to have any wish to raise their eyes from the ground, unless to answer or ask a question: all had their swords on their laps, and looked far from comfortable or at their ease in *the* presence. Our first visit was a ceremonial affair, so I quickly took my leave, asking for a private audience in future. As I left the Charbagh I was surprised to find a well-dressed and soldierly-looking company of Heratee Sepoys ready to present arms to me, which, by the way, they did very badly.

After my visit, on reaching home, I again dressed as a Persian and went for a stroll into the city. We first went to see the ark or citadel, from the top of which, being the highest point of the city, a good view is obtained of the whole of the walls and gates. All the roofs were domed; few, if any, were good buildings; all seemed poor, and the best-looking were the four covered bazaars, which, meeting in the centre, were marked by the high dome of Charsue, or "place of four roads." The mosques in the city are few and mean, no fine domes or minars to mark their site, and the walls, though of great height, look forsaken and out of repair. The ark, situated at the northern corner of the walls, is a large mound on which several rooms have been built, and is surrounded by a wall of its own; a broad ramp leads to the upper court, and a small battery crowns all, but is not armed. The whole is surrounded by a wet ditch, with a drawbridge, all of which, again, is within the city walls. From this I went along the bazaar to the Charsue, which was very crowded, it being a market-day. This is a nice walk, summer and winter, tolerably broad and well lighted, something similar to the great bazaar near the San Sofia, in Constantinople. The bazaars might be cleaner, and they did not give me the appearance of being very rich or well supplied; but on noticing this to my companions, they said it was owing to the fear the merchants had of making any great display. From this I went to see the silk quarter. Here they reel the silk from the cocoon; dye, twist, and weave it. Most of the silk is sent to Meshed and Cabul in the shape of yarn, as their piece-goods are not of any value.

On going home to the mid-day meal, or *nahr*, I found a sumptuous meal awaiting me—two large trays, *tash*, had been sent from Yakoob Khan's kitchen, from which I was feasted daily. One contained meats of various sorts—sweet, sour, savoury, greasy, dry, &c., all in little bowls, or *kosa*, with some also containing soup; and in the centre was a very large pile of rich *pillao*, without which no Afghan dinner is complete. Amongst other good things, I must not forget *koorot*. This curious article of food is made out of curds slightly salted, rolled up into balls, and dried, which keep for a long time, and is used both at home and on the road by all classes; this, broken up in a bowl of milk or water, and eaten with the usual *nan*, or flat cake, and *rognee*, or fat, is far from bad. The second tray had twelve bowls of sweets and fruits, raw and cooked, all finished up with some bunches of delicious grapes from the royal gardens. The season for them being just over, these had been cut and hung up in a large cool place, made on purpose: and in this manner grapes are preserved all the winter. In the evening I had several people in to get information from—silk merchants, *shroffs*, money changers —from whom I bought many curious coins of the neighbouring countries, as well as ancient ones found in the ruins of the old city of Herat, besides listening to Shere Mahomed's stories of the chequered career of his master.

Next morning I went for a ride outside the walls. They have been so often knocked down and rebuilt—in 1833 by Prince Abbas Mirza, and the last time by the Persians, during the siege in 1856, when it was taken, and its chief, Mahomed Yusuf, sent to Teheran and murdered—that the present ones are built on the top of a high mound of vast thickness, the accumulated *débris* of a hundred generations. The ditch is very deep and broad, and can be filled with water from the river at a short notice. There are five gates, all of which are on a level with the country outside, consequently much lower than the actual walls. The ark stands out very prominently; and on the outer slope of the mound, between the ditch and the walls, are two covered ways, or *fausscbraye*, one commanding the other; and lastly, the walls themselves are well flanked by large bastions—a place of vast strength when protected by a resolute garrison. The circumference of the city is about a farsak, the interior nearly a mile square. It is commanded by two elevations about 800 to 1000 yards distant, Mosulla and Thalehberghy; but from neither can the interior of the city be actually seen, they being only on a level with the walls. Both these elevations are covered with ruins and remains of forts; and the former, with the magnificent ruins of the mosque and tomb of Sultan Hussein Mirza Bairam, one of the house of Timour, of the fifteenth century (1498), the elegant minars of which I saw long before I arrived at this city, and said to have been partially destroyed by Chengis Khan.

Such is the fort of which Yakoob Khan has been master so long. Here, in June 1863. on the death of Dost Mahomed Khan—shortly after he had taken Herat from Sultan Jan, who had invaded his territory by taking Furrah—his eldest son, Shere Ali, set off for Cabul to take possession of the throne, leaving his own son Yakoob, sixteen years of age, as Governor of

Herat. In 1867 Herat, as also Cabul, was taken by Afzul Khan, the Ameer's uncle. Shere Ali and his sons became fugitives, the former to the north, the latter to the south. After many days' wanderings, one as far as Meshed, and with great privations, Yakoob Khan, with a small band of followers, again entered the Herat district, and being joined by about a thousand swordsmen, began to retake the villages in the neighbourhood. After Ghorian had fallen to him he found many adherents, owing to his growing fame as a gallant soldier and generous chief. He stormed Herat with about 5000 men, and took the place by a masterly *coup de main*, assisted no doubt by treachery within the garrison. Having become master of the whole country in 1868, he assisted his father with men and money to retake Candahar in April, and Cabul in September, 1868, and thus showed himself a loyal subject of his father—not the rebellious young scamp the Cabul Sirdars are trying to prove him, and which his father (infatuated by the love he bears for the mother of Abdoolla Jan, Yakoob's younger half-brother) is willing to believe, in the hopes of being able to deprive Yakoob of his birthright as heir apparent to the throne of Cabul.

I again went to the bazaars to purchase more gold in exchange for my Persian silver; also obtained more coins. The whips (*kamcheen*) of this place are famous, being beautifully plaited raw hide. Rode on to see the beautiful mosque of Mosulla, the ruins of which are covered with beautiful glazed blue and gilt tiles, and the texts from the "Koran," which appear over the arches, are of a kind the execution of which is simply marvellous. I have never seen better. The gate of the Mosulla is something like that of the archway to the mosque of Gowhur Shad at Meshed, as far as I could remember; but, as I could not get very close to the Holy Gate, I cannot say if the tiles are quite of the same description.

After several previous interviews, on my last day's stay I again went to see him, and bid adieu to Yakoob Khan, and found him alone with Sirdar Mahomed Hussein Khan; they were by the open window, looking on at some recruits drilling in the square. On my entrance the Sirdar took his place in front, and I on Yakoob's *furrush*. This time I took the opportunity of speaking about the depredations committed by the *Alamans*, and told him that the Hasameh Sultanat of Meshed had des if he did not think that a combined effort on the part of Persia and Herat could put a stop to this distressing state of things. The Prince said that he had done all he could to prevent it, but accused Yakoob of not being equally zealous in the cause, and that the nearer tribes of Turkomans could be influenced by him if he wished. Yakoob's answer to this was that he punished the *Alamans* when they came on his territory, but the Persians were afraid of them, and the *Alamans* were tempted by the half-hearted measures of the Kajar's Kafir* Government, who used to declare that the *Alamans* were allowed to go along the Herat border till they had passed Karez and Tybut, and then they used to raid on Persian soil. "As if," said Yakoob, "I would allow those thieves to come into my country if I could help it. The truth is they use both countries alike, but I am more on my guard than the Persians. At the same time I am trying to make some arrangements with the Turkos, and hope in time to mitigate these evils, which injure my people as much as the Persians."

* The Persians are called unbelievers by all sects of Sunnis. They used to be Sunnis also, previous to Nadir Shah's time, but he turned the nation in

What he said about the fear the Persians had of the Turkomans is perfectly true, and it is only their arrant cowardice that renders Turkistani raids so prevalent. The last defeat the Persian army sustained from the Tekke Turkomans was in 1860, when their army was decimated, besides losing thirty guns (afterwards recovered).

Yakoob is very desirous to re-establish Kafir Killa, the frontier post, but has not sufficient population even for the Kohsan district. After tea and pipes were brought in, he began to speak to me in broken English about the troubles in his family, saying he was his father's most loyal servant, but the intrigues at Cabul, and the enmity between the Ameer's and his councillors and people, was so great, that although Lord Mayo had done all he could for him in trying to reconcile him to his father, it was of little good. "I know," he said, "the very fact of my speaking to you in your language will be reported at Cabul, and will be put down to me, as hatching some intrigue against my father." I asked him why he did not come and visit India, like his father. He said—"I should be most happy to do so, and have often desired to go and see the *tumasha* of India, but do not dare to leave my government, lest in my absence it might be given to my younger brother, Abdoolla." He asked me if I had seen his armoury and gun foundry. On this I tried to explain to him that the duty of a good ruler was not to give all his attention to his army, but also to encourage trade and agriculture, make roads, and protect traffic, &c. &c. "I know," he said in Persian, "you English desire trade and peace, and that your wealth comes from your good arrangements; but I have first to secure my seat here by force of arms, before I can think of aught else. Herat is very poor, and I can hardly hold my own; but in me you have a well-wisher to your Government, and, if possible, I shall copy their policy." Here I made him understand about my not being on Government duty, and that anything I said was not of an official description, but only to show my personal friendship.

Having parted with him I went and saw his guns and rifles—six new smooth-bores, six-pounders, well made and mounted, besides a lot of small old guns; his rifles were roughly made, but looked serviceable. On reaching home I found a fine horse and pony sent as presents by Yakoob; both these I returned, with thanks.

The forces at his disposal are six regiments of about a thousand men each, two of which are regularly drilled and armed, while the other four are not so well cared for as yet, for want of means. The cavalry are numerous, of a very motley description, and quite undisciplined. In case of war he might have eight to ten thousand men of all arms. Their physique is good. Each gets 10 krans, about six shillings, besides food and uniform, per month; the cavalry the same, also food for their horses. Besides that part of the army which is paid, there is another which answers to our militia; these render military service for the lands they hold in *Teool*, or jagheer; and as an immense proportion of the Herat district, which is divided into four counties —Ghorian, Koorkh, Shaufbaun, and Honbeh—is *Teool*, poor Yakoob loses a large portion of revenue, which, if the country were quiet, could be let on lease to the Crown, and so brighten his pecuniary prospects.

I left this place, with regret, by the Candaharee Darwaza, through which Nadir Shah entered with his vast Delhi loot, in 1739. All was so novel and interesting, and I should have liked to have become better acquainted with Yakoob Khan. He is a very rising man, and will one day become of great importance. If the British Government do not foster him as he deserves (he is one who will turn out of quite another stamp to his father), they will regret it when too late. Now he is young, with a mind capable of taking good impressions, which ought to be forced on him by the gentle pressure of personal influence. If he should become soured by neglect and unfair treatment at the hands of his father, and we do nothing to uphold him, then we may expect his bitter hatred, and of this I am certain—from his character and from the accounts of his influence in this part of the country—that he will not tamely submit to be deprived of his natural rights; and in case of his younger brother, Abdolla Jan, being made heir to the throne of Cabul, if Yakoob does not succeed in taking the country by force of arms, he, at least, will receive such support from his own people that the state of Herat will be again torn from the kingdom of Cabul. We shall again see Abdool Rahman, Esah Khan and Co., as candidates for, at least, a portion of Afghanistan—viz., Balkh and Kundooz; and the rest of the country will be in as great a state of anarchy as before Dost Mahomed's time—which God forbid. At Afzul Khan's death, we ought to have tried to get his son and nephew into our keeping, instead of letting them go over into Russian protection. Abdool Rahman, after wandering in Khorasan, went to Bokhara, and at last, in 1870, was pensioned by General Kauffmann; he now lives at Samarcand. He is married to a daughter of Jehandar Shah, the ex-Ameer of Badakshan, who was dethroned by the help of Cabul in 1873, so that two discontented families are now allied.

One other fact I wish to point out is that, at the present moment, Yakoob thinks highly of us and has instructed himself in the English language, and, in my humble opinion, he of all other Afghans is the most susceptible to personal influence. Then let him feel the invigorating warmth of our friendship; let him have the opportunity of conversing with some high-minded English gentleman; let him have the advantage of his wild thoughts and ideas being directed into that channel in which, of all others, we should most like to see them fixed—viz., a real friendship to the British Government, and the advantages of a peaceful reign. In Russian hands he will become a most dangerous weapon against us.

Herat is situated in a broad valley, four miles from the hills to the north and about twelve to the hills south of it. This large valley is watered by canals from the Hurri Rood, which is dammed up by a *bund* thrown across it a few miles above the city. One of the many water-courses enters the city, others water the whole plain, which, if the country were quiet, would be one large sheet of cultivation. As the land is fertile and the climate good, a few years would turn all this desert into a garden!

HERAT TO CANDAHAR.

Subzewar and its Chief—Provisions for the Journey—Nomades and their Tents—Cross the Boundary of Herat—Long March—Change Escort—Furrah, City in Ruins—Garrison under Arms—Sheep Tax—Sakee and Dilaram—Seistan Boundary—Murder of Feramoze—Merchants heavily Taxed—A Feast on Carrots—Girishk and the Helmund—Reach Candahar.

OUR first stage, after leaving Herat, was Mir Daood, an old serai at the mouth of the pass through the hills which stretch between Herat and Subzewar. We marched rapidly over the horrid country, inhabited by Noorzaies, a perfect desert of hills, ruins, and no water—the results of the cruelty and oppression of years. The traces of the British were often visible, not only in the gates of Herat, especially the Durwaza Mullik, through which I had entered, but also in the ruined serais on this road, such as Shah Beg, Mir Ollah, Khoja Ooreh, &c., on all of which have been left some small signs of our handy work; but all are now in such ruin that it requires some search to distinguish one sort of work from another. Over these hills the wind was very cold, and already the highest peaks of the Hazara mountains were seen covered with snow. As we debouched into the plain of Subzewar (called Jamberan) on the third day, we had the pleasure of seeing cultivation again, with large flocks and herds. Within a few miles of this fort the road is good again, which in the hills was very rough. This is a pretty little plain surrounded with hills, on which latter roam vast flocks of ibex and markhor, the horns of which the natives use to ornament their graves. I saw several heads larger than Cashmere can boast of, which were mostly killed on the snow.* The Governor of this place, Sirdar Peer Mahomed Khan, Populzaie, has little or no influence with the Hazarees, Noorzaie, and Zooree tribes; he only collect rents, and is an old man who has travelled in Peshawur and Lahore. He is also Yakoob Khan's father-in-law, by whose daughter the Sirdar has a child.

The Subzewar district extends to Jedge or Zeje, on a small river, the Adreshkan, which rises at Kulla Khushk, at the upper part of the valley. We crossed it at Adreshkan on the second day, where another stream joins it, called the Roodiguz, beyond

* When the snow lies thick on the ground the people surround a herd, which, not being able to get away, owing to their small feet sinking in the snow, are soon disposed of

which, on the left bank, commences the Furrah district. This river flows down into Seistan, but only in the spring, during the floods, where it goes by the name of Heroot or Harood.

I must not omit to mention the kind way in which Yakoob Khan had provided for my journey to Furrah. He had sent a cook, with four yaboos of provisions. carpets, &c., for my use, besides giving me an escort up to the limits of his government, which ends at Jedge; but they went with me even as far as Furrah, to spare me all the trouble they possibly could. Formerly the Furrah district used to be under the Herat Government, but since Shere Alli's time, owing to his jealousy of his son, it has been made into a separate velayat. At the death of Shah Kamran, in 1843, the Herat authority used to extend to Washere.

Leaving Subzewar over the Kotul, under the ancient rock fortress of Killa Dookhter, a ruined fort on the left of Adreshkan, where the river turns the hills—the other ruin, Killa Pissur, is on the bank opposite—we wended our way over a rocky road to Durwazaie, which is inhabited by mixed Dooranees, Goorazais, and Noorzaie clans, and encamped with a tribe of Eleots in a small dell, near water brought from a newly-dug *karaiz* close by. They cleared out two of their tents for me, and were very civil, and greatly enjoyed their durbar with the *Inglese dowlut.* These black goat-hair tents are quite comfortable: one end is portioned off for the people, then comes the hearth, always with a fire and a cast-iron pot (Russian) on it of hot water for tea, beyond which are tethered the sheep or cattle, all helping to keep one another warm in the cold weather; and when that is verv severe they build a low wall inside the tent, which is pegged down outside it, and keeps out all the wind. They are often thirty by twenty feet, but mostly twenty by ten feet, and five and a half feet high. These wanderers speak Persian, and do not like to live in houses, because of the fear of oppression. When the taxes are too heavy for them to bear, they take flight during the night with bag and baggage, wives and little ones, without having given the slightest indication of their approaching departure. They own large flocks of goats, sheep, and camels, also a few horses and bullocks, often changing their quarters in search of pasturage; but these tribes all have some one district where they grow their crops, and for which they have to pay heavy water-rates, which is often the only way of taxing them. Mullik Gaffoora, their chief, an old man, no better than most of them in appearance, looks after one hundred tents, with five or six hundred people. Their women weave clothes and carpets, and help in making tents.

Between Subzewar and Furrah there are no villages—a vast jumble of valleys and hills, with small plains, inhabited only by a nomadic people. Each place has its name, but if the traveller finds tents at the same place twice he is very lucky. E. Conolly, who passed this in August, 1839, says it was green with grass (!) but unfit for cattle. The Afghan calls all places *abad*, or inhabited, if they even have a tent or a drop of water, and I should have fared as badly as M. Ferrier, in 1845, if it had not been for Yakoob Khan's kindness. Next day we followed the stream to Kilamoosha, only a few black tents. Here the river goes through the hills, but we cut off the bend by going over them direct by a good road to Jedge, where we found the Adreshkan again. This place (there being no permanent village there, but only tents) is the farthest point of the Hèrat territory, and to this point Yakoob Khan had told his servants to conduct me, and had given them a letter to the

Governor of Furrah to send an escort to Jedge to take charge of me; but on my arrival there I found no one, any more than I had at Kaffir Killa, on the western frontier of Herat. We here left the country of the Noorzaies, and entered into that of the Atchakzaies. Having come already a long march, I wanted to stay the night here; but the people were unwilling to take us in, saying they had nothing to give us to eat, so we were obliged to start off again through newly-ploughed fields, for a second march as long as the first, over hills and along the valley of Khoos. When half-way there the sun went down without any signs of habitation being seen. After struggling on for more than two hours we luckily saw some lights, and after nearly breaking our necks down wells and over rocks, we found them to belong to a tribe of Eimucks, who had just pitched their camp, as the place afforded food for their camels—thorns. They kindly took us in, but it was not till midnight that we were able, dead tired as we were, to lie down. If it were not for the luck of finding these tents we should have camped out and starved, as we had no provisions left, having had only a few dates to eat all day. On these occasions I found great comfort from

Liebig's extract of meat, drinking it as a weak infusion, like tea. Distance to-day, twelve farsaks.

On leaving Khoos we passed through a gorge in the hills, and came out into the Furrah plain. Here, in the distance, I saw a cloud of dust and horsemen rapidly approaching us, who proved to be my escort. Having dismounted, we spread a carpet and seated ourselves on it, and went through the usual salutations prior to Shere Mahomed Khan and his Heratees taking their leave of me. I gave them a receipt for my safety as far as this, and a few *ashurfees.* We parted mutually satisfied, though I regretted parting from Shere Mahomed, he being a well-bred young fellow, different from the boors who were to be my companions for the future. They were quite ready to go back to Jedge the same day, a distance of nearly sixty miles. These horsemen in general are very hardy, and go long distances. For instance, when Yakoob Khan retook Herat, in 1868, this same young man rode with the news to Cabul in nine days, and returned in twelve, all on the same horse, a distance of 220 farsaks each way, which, taking the farsak at three and a half miles, equals about eighty-five miles a day going there. Greater feats have often been performed by the *Alamanees* when pushed by pursuit.

Far in the distance on this desert plain we saw the ruins of an old fort, Khakee Sufed, beyond which we went to the village of Dookin, where the sowars lived, a couple of farsaks from Furrah, a poor village of shepherds, who cultivate a few fields. These people had sent two *chappaus*, or raids, into Seistan this year, and stolen cattle and sheep as reprisals for others stolen by the Belooches last year. This is the first set of raids for several years since the time of Kamram of Herat, who was murdered in 1844, and his minister, Yar Mahomed Khan, afterwards ruler till 1851. In former days the Furrah road used to be *chappaod* by Belooches on their riding-camels or *badees*, which, carrying two men each, would suddenly appear in a district, loot all they could, and be off again into the trackless waste, where water was only known to themselves.

I was entertained as well as I could be by these poor people, having to drink sheep's milk, as there were no cows in the village. Next morning a few ragged horsemen showed me over the marshy plain bordering the Furrah Rood, which we crossed to the city of Furrah. This river runs into Seistan, and is dry for three parts of the year; but in spring it must be quite two hundred yards broad if it fills its banks. There is no cultivation round the city, not even up to the walls; lots of ruins only.

The appearance of Furrah, a short way off, is imposing. Its high embattled and bastioned walls, its broad, well-kept ditch, and fine large gate and drawbridge, give it the air of wealth and ease. But what a delusion this is! Misery and desolation are its portion. This was the birth-place of Rustum, the Persian Hercules. On entering the city, I was astonished to see its fallen state. The size of the interior is, perhaps, the third of Herat; but it does not possess above twenty huts, and those all in ruins. Where is the city of Furrah? Nowhere!

Sirdar Abdoolla Khan received me civilly, and we had a short interview on the roof of his wretched abode. When it was all over, they led me into a miserable hut, in the midst of heaps of ruins—a guest-house not fit to keep dogs in. Shortly after I was settled, in came a large dish from the Sirdar, of the usual *pillao*, with a few fruits, &c.—a better dinner than I had been having lately. This Abdoolla, a Mahomedzaie Barakzaie, is the son of Sirdar Meer Afzul Khan, a Durani, son of Purdil Khan, and uncle of Ameer Dost Mahomed Khan. Some call him a tyrant. He is *locum tenens* for his father, at present at Cabul (having been called there to settle his accounts). He is thirty years old, dark, with a long face—a tall, but neat-looking man. He is married to the Ameer Shere Ali's sister, by whom he has two sons and one daughter. He has other wives besides. Shere Ali is also married to his sister—a double relationship—and she is the mother of Abdulla Jan.

Next day I did not see the Sirdar again before starting, but had the horses reshod, and got away with a few ragged sowars, as miserably armed and mounted as was the condition of their city, which dates its utter ruin from the time that Mahomed Shah, Kajar besieged Herat, in November, 1837 (Pottinger's time). A ten months' siege, when the Candahar chief Purdil Khan took away all its population to aid the Shah. Also, in 1852, Kohundil Khan, his brother, seized it and laid waste all he could, because it belonged to Herat, which was then in the hands of the Persians, its Governor being Syad Mahomed Khan, son of Yar Mahomed Khan, before mentioned.

We soon left all signs of cultivation or habitation behind, and entered a stony valley, and then, over a low pass, we advanced over one of the numerous plains that form this country, which stretched away to the south, towards Seistan, in unbounded desolation; rocky hills cropped up on all sides, in sharp, isolated peaks; the road itself is level and good. We saw plenty of antelope near the stage of Khormalik. This place is situated in a small grassy hollow. A few date palms and cattle, in the immediate neighbourhood of a few mean huts and a wall-surrounded tower, are all it possesses. As we approached we saw a few heads over the top of the tower, and could distinguish the flash of bright rifle-barrels in the sun as they took aim at us. At two hundred yards distance we challenged them in the Sirdar Abdoollah Khan's name to let us in, which after a short parley they did. I ascended to the top of the little mean tower to look at their weapons, and found they were old matchlocks, only one being in a serviceable condition. So poor a place could give us nothing; and I was thinking how I should get a meal, when the alarm was again sounded by the women, and up the men rushed to the tower to see who was the enemy.

They turned out a godsend to me. The Sirdar I had just left, though poor enough, had kindly sent me his negro Nazir, or head servant, with a cook and scullion, and a stock of provisions to comfort me on my dreary road to Washere. The nights are generally still, with no wind, both in Khorasan and this country, during this time of the year, which was fortunate for me, as here I obtained little shelter. The heat had greatly increased during the day, since passing Khakee Sufed, as we were in the lower plain country which extends to Seistan, and generally called Zumindwar. It is a great sheep-grazing district; they and camels only seem to thrive. After a long day's march without water, we encamped at Bukhwa, a small collection of huts and tents, which gives its name to the vast plain which surrounds it. Wherever water appears there is an encampment; but it is scarce. Last year Furrah was again deserted for want of water, the sheep and camels all being driven down towards Seistan, at the risk of being attacked by the Seistanees. Each sheep gives an income to its owner of a kran (six annas = eightpence), and each camel about two krans, half of which is taxed by the Government.

Next day was the Mussulman Eed, and I was destined to remain on this dismal plain for another day, moving from Bukhwa to Sakee, a farsak distant, with only tents to live in—not the *kharga* or framed circular sort, but of black blanket, and oblong. The people said that the next two marches ahead I should get nothing to live on for either men or horses, and that forage must be collected and taken on.

At Sakee the Malik Abdool Rizzak Khan, Candaharee came out for the *istikbal*.* He told me there were two hundred Kheyls or large families on this plain, scattered far and wide at the different waters, with large flocks of camels, sheep, goats, and oxen. I obtained a few coins, here said to be Belooch, or Seistanee. Having taken on with us next day the barley and *kah*, or chaff, required for the next marches, collecting which, was the real reason of my delay here, we started—a large party, made up of merchants and chance travellers, who had helped to swell my party, for the sake of protection. Our mounted escort rushed over the plain, charging one another, firing off their *jezails* and *tofungs*, and seemed to go generally mad along

* The ceremony of welcoming a guest.

the plain. Crossing the dry bed of the Ibraheen Joee, and a few *karez*, we arrived at the right bank of the Kashrood, which stream rises a long way off in the high mountains of Seah Koh, but now nearly dry, which we followed till we arrived at the old ruin of Dilaram,* a fort built sixty years before by a Hindoo; now only half a tower is left, where we found some wild-looking Achakzaie runners to carry the mail between Herat and Candahar. The river bed, here broad, is covered with a dense tree jungle, which looked lovely in its autumnal colouring.

This jungle, to how many, has it not been a slough of despond? For opportunities lost in not crossing over at once—for loitering in its green shady nooks—has often led to capture and death from some Belooch *chuppaws* and ambuscades, as they and their long-legged riding camels lay quietly waiting for their prey. The other, or left bank, again takes up the same desolate appearance; and to the north were the distant Hazara Mountains. The plains to the south are nearly impassable for horses after a heavy shower of rain, the hard soil becoming like grease,

* Heart's ease.

giving no foothold; but this is a rare occurrence, as rain does not often fall here. An instance is given —when Mahmood Shah, that very unlucky monarch, and his son, Kamran, were flying before the victorious Candaharee Sirdars in December of 1825 a shower caught them on this plain, and nearly caused their capture. This is the most southern point of Afghanistan proper towards Seistan, consequently the most disturbed, raids on both sides being the usual occupation. The people only water their flocks every other day; so, often they do not know till the evening of the second day if a flock has been captured, as the poor shepherds are generally taken off too, so as not to spread the alarm.

I may as well mention here the description given of the Seistan Boundary Commission in 1872.* I do not vouch for its truth, but it was told me by one of Sir Frederick Goldsmid's servants, and the people in these parts all believe the same story :—

"I went with my master to Seistan, to the town of

* The settlement of the boundary between Persia and Afghanistan, in the Seistan district, caused at this time a great stir in the country, but it was finally agreed to by the rulers of both States. See Note at p. 166.

Jooaim, held by Sirdar Mahomed Ali Khan. Another town is Lash, the Governor of which is Sirdar Sultan Ahmed Khan. Shureef Khan Belooch has a fort of his own. Taj Mahomed Khan has another fort, but is now imprisoned at Teheran. The Sahib was six days at Jooaim before the General Sahib (Pollock) joined him. As soon as the General arrived from Candahar with all his *fouj* or escort of cavalry and infantry, the Persians refused them any sort of provisions, even for money, so it had to be brought from Furrah, four days off. We all remained here together four days, when, not getting any supplies, we marched for Meshed, which we reached in twelve days. The Sahibs, I knew, were Goldsmid, Pollock, Bellew, Lovatt, Smyth, and Synd Noor Mahomed Shah.* When we arrived at Meshed, the Vakeel (agent) of the Dowlut Inglese (British Government) failed to obtain money for the Sahibs, wanting a kran for each toman, commission, but Mirza Abbas Khan† got them all they required, and he was made the Vakeel."

* The Afghan Envoy, who died during the Conference at Peshawur, in May, 1877.

† My friend at Meshed.

The Malik of Sakee left me next day at Dilaram, or "Heart's ease," he going back home and I on towards Washere—a horrid long march; over rough ground, covered with a very large description of gravel. Most of the way lay along the stream Kashrood, the heat being unbearable. This, and most other Khorasan streams, have *bands* or dams, thrown across their beds during the dry season—viz., nine months—to catch all the water they can for irrigation purposes. As we neared Washere, we came across the streams from *karez*, and small wells. The village is mostly of tents. The army that returned from Furrah to Candahar had nearly ruined the place; they had eaten off all the barley, so our quads only got wheat. The above army, commanded by General Feramoze Khan, a Mahomedanised Kaffir, Yakoob's inveterate enemy, and Commander-in-Chief of the Cabul Forces, was sent to Furrah by the Ameer, Shere Ali Khan, to intimidate his son, Yakoob Khan. They halted at Furrah for eight months, in 1870, during which time Feramoze Khan was murdered (by Aslum Khan, half-brother to the Ameer, who was in his turn murdered by his two younger brothers while a prisoner at Cabul), after which the army broke up and returned—having done nothing except engaging in a few skirmishes!

I knew Aslum Khan well when he was in Peshawur in 1866. To us he was a very pleasant man. The Malik told me that a month ago the Ameer had sent orders to have 200 camels collected for the transport of a large force to Seïstan, to settle the boundary question. Thanks to our interference, this will now remain an open sore in the sides of both Persian and Afghan. From all I can hear, Afghan forces predominate there.*

Malik Mahomed Oosman Khan, Noorzaie gave me a tent and food, but the *rogun*, or fat, was very rancid—famous, as he called it! From Subzewar I had been joined by several people, merchants, &c., going to Candahar. From one of these men I heard a good deal of the cruel manner in which they have to pay toll on all merchandise. For instance, all goods entering the city of Candahar have to pay the octroi duty *ad valorem*, and, when anything is taken out of the city for sale in the interior, they again have to pay

* Now we know better; and, thanks to Sir Fred. Goldsmid's exertions, order has been established. The above remarks were written in 1873.

twenty-five Candaharee rupees (twelve annas each) per camel load—at Girishk three and a half krans (six annas each) per load; again at Furrah one-fortieth of the value of each load; and at Herat one-thirtieth of the value, besides a few krans here and there to any one who has the power of enforcing black mail *en route*. While waiting for all my party to get ready, so as to start together, a burly *faqueer* with a spear, on the top of which was a large bunch of black wool, came close to me, shouting "*Huk! huk!*" and stuck it into the ground at my feet, and would not leave till I gave him some money! Such is the insolence of these beggars.

My Furrah escort having returned from here, I was quite at the mercy of the small Maliks on the road, also of passing travellers always glad to find plunder, and therefore on the look-out for it. My trading companions and servants were very uneasy at the prospects of travelling without some protection, especially as, when we should near Candahar, more people would be met on the road. I only had two wild horsemen as guides. They were mounted on ponies, and armed with large bell-mouthed carbines, swords, and brass-bossed shields; and these left us at Ikling, the first village from Washere, having gone two farsaks only. Near Ikling, close to the road, is a curious stone pillar, of which I could learn nothing.* Our guards, instead of getting some one to take their place, quietly pointed to the village and disappeared: thus we were left alone, to find out the road as well as we could. The road lay over and between low hills, with but one watering-place *en route*. I saw many flocks of sheep; and it is a marvel on what they live—all looked so parched and dry, producing only Artemisia, Saltworths, and Camelthorn. After hours of plodding we came on to the plain again, and far on the horizon saw some black tents at Beobanak. These *eliots* had arrived here a few weeks before, and had only just finished clearing out the *karez*, so had nothing to offer us but an old fowl, and part of a tent, shared with their oxen. Next morning was very cold, as we left the tents and passed between the two hills which divide this from the Girishk country. The road goes over a level country to Mahmoodabad, a very small village in a hollow, watered by a *karez*. Here we purchased some nice young carrots from the villagers, and most delicious

* It was evidently ancient, and deserves the notice of antiquarians.

they tasted to me, after such a continuance of *pillao*, and *pillao* only. This national dish of the Afghans consists of greasy rice, and is eaten with or without meat. A few farsaks farther, over an undulating and sterile plain, we reached the old fort of Saadut, built by Dost Mahomed's brother, Khoondil Khan; it seemed quite deserted, and I should like to have stayed and investigated this old ruin, but night was approaching and the way long, so I galloped on and rejoined my silent companions. All were eagerly looking out for the towers of Girishk, hoping to see them from every ascent; but it was long after dark that we saw a solitary light, which guided us off the plateau we had been traversing down into the valley of the Helmund. At so late an hour it was with difficulty we gained admittance into the fort, entering half drowned from the deep ditch we had to ford, the guards being too lazy to let down the drawbridge for us. I found the Khan away, but his son was good enough to share his evening meal with me. This was Futteh Khan Barukzai's fort, eldest son of Poyndah Khan, the Barukzai chief who supported Timour Shah and Zeman Shah, and brother to Dost Mahomed, and uncle to the present Ameer, Shere Ali. He was Vizier to Mahmood Shah, who, jealous of his power and influence, first blinded, then murdered his benefactor, to whom he owed his throne, in 1810.

We were a large party, stuffed into a small room with a huge fire, and the door shut. I asked to have it open, but they all objected, saying the Inglese were too particular, and that I ought to have learnt to accommodate myself to all situations. The worst of it was they had a young tame deer, which would share my carpet, and kept me awake half the night. The morrow being Sunday, I halted here for the day.

The fort is in a very dilapidated condition, but there are still many marks left of our occupation of it by Sir Henry Rawlinson, in a gate and bastion. From the top of the walls a good bird's-eye view is obtained of the surrounding villages, also of the ruined Fort Nadali opposite, and the river beyond. The situation of the fort is elevated, built on a rise on the banks of the Helmund, which here forms a valley, called Ghurrum-seil, and about one mile broad, populated by the Noorzai Kheil. As far as the water could reach, was beautifully green and fertile; the large canals coming from the river irrigated the gardens and fields, and also filled the moat round the fort.

There are only half a dozen small villages and a little bazaar outside the gate; all beyond is bleak desert. This is a very important position, commanding the road to Herat and Candahar, and the ford over the Helmund, which is generally too rapid and deep to be forded at any other point near here. The bank and sands of the river are covered with jungles full of deer, pigs, duck, and partridges. As the Malik Kadir Khan was away, the people refused to give me any one to escort us; so, leaving Girishk, off we went again all by ourselves. As we descended into the water meadows, we had to break through the ice, and our poor steeds got badly cut in crushing their way to the river bank. A young Afghan, seeing us alone, offered to show us the ford; and as we advanced we disturbed a sounder of pigs in the jungle, after which, one of the Khojahs or merchants galloped, till he was safely landed in a deep pool of slime, to the great amusement of the rest. We hesitated on the bank, as the river was rushing past very fast, clear, and cold; but the poor boy, only clad in blue cotton, manfully jumped in and drove the ponies across, we following as best we could over the slippery stones.

The Helmund is about one hundred yards broad at

this season, and three and a half feet deep, it being at its lowest, and is split up into many small streams. When the river floods, from the melting snow, it must be at least a mile broad at this point, though generally it is narrow and deep; it is at its highest in the end of May, or the beginning of June. All our traps became quite wet, so that when we reached the top of the opposite side, which is higher than the right bank, we all sat down to lay out our things to dry. My papers luckily escaped becoming wet through, being at the top of a load. "The river hugs the left bank, and seemingly has deserted the right, and is still undermining the cliffs in the south. I do not know if it is ever navigated by rafts, or how far a raft could go down towards Seistan." This remark of Conolly's is true now. After half an hour's drying we started again, gladdening the heart of the boy by a kran. The road lay again over the stony, sandy desert, with slight undulations, without a drop of water, and a hot sun. The Khakrez range rose behind us as we jogged on; the usual mirage showed us beautiful trees and hills and flowing streams. We reached Miskarez, a little village, at sundown. Here we had only liquid mud to drink, and that quite salt. Next day saw us nearly dead from thirst; but as we heard of a small well farther on, we moved off with hopeful hearts, and as the sun began to get hot again came to the well we had been so longing for, and found it salt! So, with drooping heads, we set off again; it seemed to me the longest day I had ever spent. Tired and feverish, I thought the camp would never come. At last, near evening, we saw a small ridge of hills, and shortly after some men rode out to meet me from the village of Aushukan, on the banks of the Candahar river, Urgundao. This *istikbal* was truly grateful, as they brought us water, knowing that that would be more welcome than aught else. This they carried under their horses, fixed to the saddle-girths.* The river runs close under the hills away to the south, and is well cultivated along its banks, though the plain is quite a desert, sloping gradually down to the river. Lots of people came out to welcome me, and I found large quantities of sweets and fruits had been sent me from Candahar.

* In leather bags, the porous nature of which induces evaporation, thereby keeping the contents tolerably cool, for a temperature of 110°.

Here my lead-pencil gave out—how long will the ink last? One of the first duties to be performed on arrival, and while waiting for my food, was to write up my journal, which performance generally caused a slight suspicion as to my motives, and I generally tried to do this in private.

CANDAHAR TO BOLAN PASS

Hospitable Reception—Enter Candahar—Afghan Troops—A Dangerous Beggar—The Authorities—Hindoos—My Quarters—The Ancient City—An Unwelcome Message—The Road Closed—Disappointments—Copper Coinage—The Ameer—I Start Southwards—My Companion—Ploughing with Camels—A Patriarchal Scene—The Pesheen Valley—Syads—The Fort of Quetta—Enter the Bolan—Difficulties of the Pass—Dadur—Among Englishmen Again—The Journey Ended—Conclusion.

THE agreeable surprise that awaited me on entering the city of Candahar raised my hopes to the utmost as to what my reception would be at Cabul. The outlying villages on the Urgundao, of which Aushukan was one, are "only" sixteen miles from the city, and it was here they began to feast me. I was awoke in the morning by a great noise outside my door, and called to my servant to find out its cause. He said that some Sirdars had arrived from the city with presents from the General and the Governor. Having dressed, I went out to meet them, and found the court into which my room led filled with bowing men and large trays of sweets, flowers, and fruits, laid out for my acceptance. I graciously condescended to receive them! and making the sign to my men, everything was quickly removed, and, of course, I never saw them again.* The Sirdar and Maliks were then invited into my room, and sat down to palaver—all to gain time to allow the troops to come out into the plain to receive me with full military honours. At this point of the journey I had not to be so strict in my disguise, and in conversing with the chiefs I openly made my remarks as an Englishman.

After an hour's delay I intimated my desire to start, so as to reach the city early, as my habit has always been to get to the end of a march as quickly as possible, and not loiter on the way. This I carried out to-day, as usual, to the great surprise of my hosts, who twice wished me to get off my horse to rest, and drink tea; and in nice spots I found carpets spread, with tea and pipes ready, so I took a cup without dismounting, at which there was a loud murmur. I had at least one hundred men with me. "What a hard soldier and accomplished traveller the Sahib Dowlut is; our Sirdars would have rested

* It is customary for the master simply to touch one of the dishes as a sign of acceptance, when they are removed and divided amongst the dependents.

three times in the same distance!" &c. &c., were the remarks I heard; and certainly when an Asiatic is well off, he does not lack in displaying the outward signs of his wealth, by having plenty of comforts around him. A few miles from the city I met the body-guard of fifty sowars sent to conduct me to where the grand *istikbal* was to take place. These men were got up in imitation of our native cavalry, and tolerably mounted on Turkoman and Herat horses. They were a troop of the Cabul regular army. They seemed gratified at my inspecting them as they were drawn up to salute me. The road was bad, owing to the many unbridged streams and watercourses that cross the country. The river Urgundao itself was very small, twenty yards broad and two and a half feet deep, as nearly all its water is taken off by canals. In all the streams I passed from Meshed, fish are scarce; those caught are captured by nets, also with poison (coculus indicus),* and are generally like a description of carp. Fish-hooks are not much used.

As I approached through the usual orchards,

* The root of the above plant is pounded and mixed up with water in a large dish, and thrown into any pool known to contain fish. They soon come to the surface, dead.

gardens, graveyards, &c., that surround an Eastern city, I saw single mounted *vedettes* flying off to give news of my approach. On the plain in front of the cantonment outside the walls I saw a grand display. General Sufder Ali Khan, in command of the Candahar forces, and the civil governor of the district, Futteh Khan, advanced in front of their deployed troops, and having dismounted, we had a hearty embrace—Afghan fashion—which was performed amidst the thunder of guns and rattle of small-arms. I could not have been received with greater honours if I had been the Shah-in-Shah or Governor-General of India.

We entered the city through the Heratee Gate and bazaar, and proceeded direct to the Ark. The streets were lined with regular troops, to keep off the crowds assembled to see me. The soldiers are most comically dressed. Their uniform, which is of an English pattern, is cut out of a striped woollen cloth that looks like bed-ticking; their trousers were too short, but well strapped down; on their heads were tall, red, conical caps, or *kullas,* with red balls dangling at the top, but no *loongees*, or turbans, giving their shaved heads a very bare, cold appearance. Their cross-belts are of brown leather, as also their pouches, and they are armed with old Tower muskets. The square in front of the Ark is a spacious one, and here the guns were parked. They appeared to be of all shapes, sizes, and dates, with carriages and limbers white with age. As I was entering the Ark gate, a dervish dashed through the soldiers and caught hold of my bridle, shouting "*Huk! huk!*" He had a knife, but did not use it, and it was not until the General, who was riding beside me, urged his horse between us, that he let go and retired, shouting "*Huk! huk!*" as before. I ought to have given him a kran, but he took me so much by surprise that I forgot to do so.*

The Ark is surrounded by a ditch on three sides, the fourth side being the north-western wall of the city. Its entrance is at the side of a vast circular bastion, from the top of which I often used to look down on the city. My residence had been prepared in the Charbagh outside the town, but I asked to be allowed to stay in the city instead; so I got an upper room, overlooking a nice garden, and not far off from

* Custom and fanaticism make these wretches most insolent, and their demand for alms is most peremptory.

where the General lived. After all the excitement was over, I was glad to find myself with the General's *mirza*, or writer, an intelligent youth of twenty-five, Ali Akbar, son of General Mahomed Hashim Khan, Kuzzulbash. We had a long talk about the affairs of the town, &c. The General Sufder Ali Khan, Kuzzulbash is a jolly, red-faced, stout, oldish man, with pleasant manners, but not very polished. He is brother to Sepa Salar Hussun Ali Khan, at Cabul. He has command of the army and town and the mint, but has nothing to do with the revenues of the country. The civil governor, Futteh Khan Atachakzaie, is a dignified, middle-aged man, with whom I had little to do. My comfortable quarters took away my aches and pains, and a *hummam* my stiffness. I did not go out all next day, but had a Hindoo *shroff* (money-changer) brought me to speak with. These men number about a thousand souls, old and young; and all live in a walled serai in the city. They are better treated now than in the olden times, but still affect great poverty, so as not to attract attention; or else they would be sure to be squeezed for a forced loan. They have lost the mild look they had in India, and have a wild, restless appearance, as if always on the look-out for danger. I got a few coins from him, and he spoke of the gold mine in the neighbourhood as a secret.* In the afternoon we had heavy rain, and I was glad of a charcoal fire in the room.† This is placed in the middle of the room in a brazier; having been well burnt outside, to take off all the bad fumes, it is brought in in a red glow.

I bought also a huge *poshteen*, or sheepskin coat, to cover me from head to foot, on my anticipated two hundred mile march to Cabul, as the *kafila* that had just arrived from there, reported the passes almost closed up with snow, and the road dangerous, as they had lost six camels down the ravines and wells, which were undistinguishable, all being filled with snow. I also sent the letters with which I had been entrusted from Meshed to their owners, and wrote to India, viâ Cabul and Peshawur, a few lines to say I was safe and well. I am well guarded by soldiers on all sides, so as to keep off loafers and beggars, who are legion, and of a most loathsome description. I could see out of my lofty look-out the hills of solid rock to

* This is now well known to exist in the hills north of the town.

† The alternations of temperature are very sudden and great, a difference often of sixty degrees in a few hours.

the east, on which was the ancient city of Candahar, first built by Babur in 1522, high upon the summits, and which was destroyed by Nadir Shah in 1740; and also could see Ahmed Shah's famous tomb. The far-reaching guns of modern science can now command the city from the south-eastern heights, but which were far out of the reach of shot during our occupation of it in 1840. Nadir Shah built a city too, which is also in ruins, and three miles to the south of the present Candahar. The present city in the plains was built by the Duranee Ahmed Shah, and whose name was retained on the coins of Dost Mahomed's early days. Ahmed Shah, the chief of the Suddozais, at the death of the Emperor Nadir Shah, became Ameer of Afghanistan, under the title of Dur-e-duram, in 1748. He also died here, in 1773; and was succeeded by his sons —Shah Zeman, Mahmud Shah, and, lastly, Shah Shuju—whom we supported, and thereby brought on the Cabul war of 1840–42. The city of Candahar is so well known already that I need not attempt to describe it, except that its narrow, winding lanes are the haunts of the grossest immorality and the worst diseases. Its last European residents before myself were the officers of Lumsden's Mission, in 1857–58

One day, while a few miles out of the city, we met the large *cortége* belonging to Mohamed Yakoob Khan's Mahomedzaie wife, and the seven women of her suite. She was carried in a red, cloth-covered litter by four men, as also were her women. They had many pony loads of property, and a large escort. She was going up to Herat to join her husband, whose position at Cabul was getting less secure Another day I heard a great firing, and on asking the cause, heard that Sirdar Mahomed Aioob Khan, Yakoob's younger brother, a lad of about fifteen, was also going up to Herat, and had then entered the city, together with Sirdar Meer Afzul Khan, of Furrah, who had been found a defaulter in his accounts up to four lakhs (40,000*l.*), and was only going back to give the government up to some one else; and this was the reason I had not seen him previously. These two went into the garden prepared for me. I am sorry I saw neither, as I was busy making up horse-clothing for the road, of thickest *numdah*.

The next day (the 14th December), early, they said the Khan wanted to see me. I told them I was not ready to receive visitors, but would be so shortly. I thought he wanted me to go and call on Aioob Khan, as he spoke of it yesterday. While I was having my morning tea he came in with the Mirza, and asked me if I had any papers to produce from the British Government, granting me permission to travel this route. I told him I had not, but that I was only travelling for my own pleasure, and not on Government duty. Then he showed me a letter just arrived by a *cossid* (carrier) from Cabul, with the Ameer's seal attached. After the usual compliments, and asking after my health, &c., it went on to say that he had heard that I was coming up to Cabul, and that he had asked the Governor-General of India, through the English Vakeel at Cabul, and the Commissioner of Peshawur, if I was travelling on any Government duty, and that they had replied, saying the officer was not travelling with Government permission or knowledge. Under which circumstances, seeing the condition of the roads and the disturbed state of the capital, he was sorry to be obliged to order the General to see that I did not take the northern road, but proceed to India viâ Quetta and Shikarpore, or Khelat. This announcement came on me like a thunderbolt; my dearly-cherished hopes were dashed to the ground. Was I not yet destined to reach that goal? I was a prey to the utmost despair for several hours. What, after all my trouble, was this to be my reward? It was a fearful pill to swallow, and it was not till the morrow I began to think of how I had arrived thus far, and who had sustained me till now. It was in a better frame of mind I thanked the Providence who had guided me, and learnt how true was the saying, "*L'homme propose, mais le Dieu dispose.*"

I went up to the top of the tower, over the square or artillery park, and took a good look round. The hills which lay to the north were reverberating with the salutes of artillery; and the troops were having a great field-day, in honour of young Aioob Khan. *On dit* he is to be Governor of Herat when Yakoob Khan gets sent up to Balkh, to prevent Abdool Rahman from carrying on any intrigue there with the help of Russian money. This is Shere Ali's great fear—losing Balkh by means of a raid by Abdool Rahman, secretly helped by Russia.*

A curious custom is prevalent in this city, which originated in the days of its former ruler, Kohundil,

* The latter part (1877) is quite as true as when I wrote it in 1873.

who died in 1855, and that is with respect to the copper coinage. Every few months the General calls in the *phool scah*, or copper money, and the people are allowed so many hours to pay it into the treasury at the current rates, getting silver in return, and next day the same copper is re-minted and issued at a higher rate. For instance, when I first arrived at Candahar it was six small coppers to one shaie, and twenty-six shaie to one kran. The day I left only five coppers went to the shaie—a gain of five shaie in each kran. When it is considered how poor the population is, all their daily wants being bought by these small phools, this direct tax is very heavily felt, but is considered by the rulers as quite a proper way of "raising the wind."

After my road to Cabul being doubly closed by Nature and by the Ameer (or rather, by our Indian Government), I did not wish to stay longer than I could help, so asked the General to let me get away as soon as possible. This he promised to do, saying he wished me to go away with honour, and he was on the look-out for a young man of *izzut* (reputation) to accompany me to Quetta. I often used to talk to the officers of my guard. They all agree that the Ameer is making too many alterations since his visit to Umballa in 1869; they do not call them improvements, which I can quite understand—one, for instance, taking away from the army their usual easy-flowing dress, and clothing them in tight coats and trousers, quite unsuited to Asiatics. The Ameer has translated the drill-book into Pushtoo, and instead of one's hearing orders in very curious English, as formerly, the men now really understand what is being said to them. The Ameer is very unpopular in Cabul, and if it were not for the money and arms supplied him by us, he would not be on the throne a month longer; it is only force that is keeping the country together. They report that he has dressed the ladies of his *anderoon*, or harem, in English muslin dresses, and taken away their veils, and wants them to go out driving in the bazaar in an open carriage, like the *Beebee Englese* (English ladies); but they are in open rebellion against him, and, like the ladies in most countries, have gained the day, anyhow for the present.

Monday (the 16th) saw me off with the same state as I had entered, the Khans taking leave of me at the gate, but the *kotwal* or mayor of the city accompanying me for some miles out of the suburbs. The young Khan that was to take me to Shawl joined here with his men, as also Hadjee, my factotum, who was going of his own accord with me, instead of remaining at Candahar. He was one of our Government pensioners, his father's property having been at our disposal during our occupation of Cabul from 1838 to 1842. Almost all persons who had been friendly to us during the war, at our departure had their houses and property confiscated by the Dost's Government, and during my stay in Persia I came across many of them, who all asked after Sir Henry Rawlinson, who formerly was so kind to them. Hadjee had left Persia with me for the purpose of seeing his friends here; and now, seeing my difficulty, kindly accompanied me.

We left the sterile hills and plains of Candahar, and dipped down into the green valley of the Doree River, which was distant about twenty miles. From Candahar to our Indian frontier they count in koss, and not in farsaks, as in Khorasan; they also use koss on the Cabul and Peshawur road. We followed the course of the river for a considerable distance; crossing our path were many canals that irrigate the lands on this or right bank; the left side is high and sandy, without cultivation. We also crossed the Turnak, a muddy slow stream, and the Arghasan; these two, together with the Musa, near Girishk, form the Argundab River, which all unite to form the Helmund. Our first halt was Tukhtapool, but we could not find it without great trouble, as it is only a small encampment among the numerous low hills about here. There was only one house, which had been lately built, and into this I got permission to enter after some difficulty, as its owner was away, and they did not like to let me in during his absence. The room proved nicely furnished, with carpets and pillows to lean against—quite an agreeable surprise in such a jungly place. Attached to the roof were horizontal beams, which they said were to hang up their winter store of meat, as they kill as many sheep as they think sufficient at the commencement of the season.* Of the next day's march the first part of the road was very stony, and through the low hills we had reached last night; then we crossed a long plain without water, but with a field here and there dependent on rain, towards another range of high hills, which divides Candahar

* These carcases remain frozen during the winter, and portions are chopped off as required for use.

from the Pesheen district. The camel is universally used to draw the plough in these parts; the whole affair is very rude, and requires two men to attend it—one to steer, and one to lead the animal.

The whole way since leaving the city we have been amongst the wild Atachakzaie tribes, once notorious robbers; but of late they have learnt such bitter lessons from the Ameer that they are getting more civilised and settling down. Each valley and water-course is owned by a different clan, a few of them living in mud huts, but most of them in their black tents. They still move about with flock and herd, as the old nomadic spirit is strong in them yet, and which they will not be able to throw off for generations, but their flittings are now confined to not more than a few miles on each side of their head-quarters. At this, our second day's camp, I had an opportunity of seeing a tribe of Afghans at home in their native wilds. The tents were here pitched half a mile from the water, which they had to go and fetch daily, the girls doing most of the hard work; the women do not veil their faces, and are a very dark, ugly race, very free and easy in their deportment, and were only prevented by the Khan from pulling about all my things, in their curiosity and eagerness to examine all I had. These people would not have robbed me there, because I was a guest; but if they had caught me outside their camp unprotected, they would most likely have taken all, and perhaps my life also.

Next morning we experienced great delay at the one well at which all the cattle were being watered, and had to fight our way to the water-trough against thirsty camels, horses, oxen, goats, and sheep, so that it was late when we again got on our way. This watering scene was most interesting, taking one back to the time of the patriarchs, for nearly the whole camp was collected here: men and women, young and old, the latter sitting on their *numdah* carpets on a slight elevation above the well, settling the disputes of the hot-blooded young ones below. As this was the only water we should find for twenty miles, we had to drink as much as we could, to counteract the great evaporation the heat would cause in our bodies.

Every mile we went towards the Bolan the heat increased, for, while it snows at Candahar, fifty miles off, in this direction it is very hot, not so much on account of the difference of altitude, but because the wind off the high land north of Candahar makes that place cold, while the low sandy plains of Beloochistan always keep this country hot. We struck the pass on the Rognee Hills in the evening after a trying march, and determined to encamp with a few *eliots* in a gorge close by. We had a most stormy meeting with these sons of the desert; they only had four or five tents, and at first point-blank refused to take us in, as they had nothing to give us to eat, but at last were induced to shelter us on the promise of payment—a most unusual thing, as these people are generally very hospitable; but these were miserably poor, hardly knowing how to live from day to day. They often eat grass boiled up with fat, and various insects, which others in a better position would think simply disgusting.

We were rather glad to get away next morning, our quarters not having been the most comfortable. We ascended the gorge by the most vile paths possible, and, after two miles, we came upon an open glade with a spring of water, called Chumuni—a place well-remembered by our army on its march on Candahar in 1838. Then our way led us up the ravines to the top of the pass—a most steep, horrid road, only fit for goats. Camels cannot cross this, but have to make a long *détour* to turn the hills to the south.

When on the top of the Kotul, we had a good view of the two plains—one north, towards Candahar, and the other south of it, the Pesheen district; but it was not an inviting sight. All had a desolate, burnt-up appearance, except a few spots where water approached the surface. Crossing at the same time with us was a *kafila* of donkeys, loaded with *rogun*, or *ghee*.* The poor little creatures were pushed about dreadfully by their cruel drivers as they urged them up, and we were glad to get away from them and the smell from their greasy loads. On the top of the Kotul we were almost cut in two by the cold wind from the Candahar direction, which below, on the plain, blew hot. The Pesheen valley, before us, had the reputation of being rich and fertile; but the first village we came to, and where we stopped for the night—Karez Inayatollah—did not appear very well off. I was detained here two days, owing to the rascality of my Khan's people, who pretended they had urgent business to transact in Candahar, the news of which they wished to get. The Khan, my companion, was a weak, tall, sallow-faced, Jewish-

* Clarified butter, universally used in the East for cooking purposes.

looking young man, Mohamed Ali Khan, son of Sirdar Mohamed Sadeek Khan, Populzaie, who is a pensioner of our Government, having helped our army by keeping the Bolan Pass clear of Murrees, Kookies, &c. The family own a small fort near Shawl, and have a certain amount of influence with the wild tribes in these parts.

This village belongs in *jagheer** to Futteh Khan, Governor of Candahar, and produces superb water-melons, which they call *Hindoowanas*, as having originally come from Hindoostan. The cooking, too, was better here than usual, the ordinary *pillao* being superseded by a rich stew, in which lentils and pease were cooked. I was greatly troubled here by the Afghans coming to me for cures for all manner of diseases—every European being looked upon as a doctor—and, as no excuses are taken, I did what I could for the poor people. They are all Syads,† and, as such, are exempt from paying taxes to their Government, but are called on, instead, to quiet the district and settle disputes between the tribes in cases of emergency. They also act as carriers; for, owing

* Freehold. † Descendants of the Prophet.

to their holy descent, they do not get looted so often as others, and are intrusted with valuable goods, such as silk and *Pushmeenas*, for the Shikarpore market, returning with indigo and English piece goods.

Across the Pesheen plain and over the Lora, a sluggish salt stream to the foot of the Shawl hills, was an uninteresting march, as also the crossing over a low range—nothing but desolation. The view of the Shawl plain was worse, if possible, than that of Pesheen. This range, though low, is important, as it forms the boundary between the territories of Khelat and Candahar. Where the crops grow is a marvel, as nothing green meets the eye; but if it were settled and irrigated, I believe no country would be richer. We could not quite reach Shawl that day, so put up at the village of Billilay. This small collection of huts is surrounded by irrigated fields, and the approach through them was very difficult, our horses sinking deep into the mud at each step. The canals which water this country come also from the Lora, but another branch from that which we crossed at first. The fort of Shawl, or Quetta, is situated at the foot of the mass of hills that extend eastward to the British frontier at Dehra Ghazee

Khan, and through which the Bolan Pass is situated. Although the elevation of the fort is about 5500 feet above the sea, still the natives all complain of its insalubrity and feverishness.

From Billilay I sent off a letter to the Khan of Khelat's Naib at Quetta, and we followed shortly after. As we approached the fort we saw the Naib Abdul Lutif and his small force turn out to do me honour. A company of the Khan's regular army is stationed here, well-dressed and armed. The fort itself is perched upon a natural mound, the foot of which is protected by a dilapidated wall and ditch. As we ascended the road that leads up to the *Killa*, we were nearly blown off our horses by their one gun, which was fired through an embrasure just above our heads. The only gate that gives access to the top of the fort is guarded by a bastion, with the gun which saluted us, and over which is the lofty balcony in which the Naib holds his durbars. Having reached the end of Mohamed Ali Khan's escort, I dismissed him with a few ashurfees, and began to make arrangements for my journey through the Bolan.

At first, on my arrival, the Naib was willing to

let me go by that route, but, receiving a letter from Candahar the next day, he began to make difficulties, saying that the Pass had been closed for months, and that several *kafilas* had been murdered and plundered; that the tribes were fighting among themselves, and that not even the *cossid* from Khelat could pass now, &c.—all of which proved to be true; but his real reason, which I got out of his Moonshee for a gold mohur,* wàs because the Candahar authorities wished me to go through Khelat, that being considered by them as the safest road. It certainly was safer, but much longer, and would have delayed me beyond my term of furlough; so I told him I was determined to go through the Bolan or Rowat Passes, either he chose—the latter goes through the Waziree country, and is little known—and, if he did not give me men to show me the way, I would go by myself.

Being well up to all the native tricks, the next morning I cleared out of the fort, and when outside, sent word to the Naib that I was waiting for his men. It was a comical sight to see him rush out and take off his turban to try and persuade

* An Indian coin, worth about thirty shillings.

me to remain. He told me the next day he would give me a large escort, with supplies, and that I was mad to go by myself, &c. But, seeing I would not return, he at last said that if I gave him a letter to the Khan, his master, saying I was determined to go through the Pass, against his wishes, it being unsafe, he would let me have a few men to go with me as far as Dadur. This letter I gladly gave him, and started immediately after, telling him to send the men to "Serab"—a place so called from its being the spring from which the stream called Shadeezaie rises, between the Umbar and Zanzeera ranges of hills--a village fifteen to twenty miles from the mouth of the Pass. *En route* there, I passed the enclosed British burial-ground of 1839–40; also the ruins of one of the houses built by the English. My reason for making such haste was, to push through the Pass before any one from Quetta had time to give information to the Murrees or other tribes in the Pass.

From Serab we started again at midnight, fifteen men having joined me: this was to enable us to get to the mouth of the Pass before daylight, so as to begin its passage at dawn.

A cold wind and cloudy sky brought in the 26th

December, so we warmed ourselves by making fires of the *jowassa*, or Camelthorn, on the Dustbedowlut plain, in front of the Pass; and, just as day dawned, crossed over the bar at the mouth, called Kharlaki, and descended into the Bolan.

The difficulties of this route naturally are very great, but when the *kafilas* and unarmed travellers are forced to hurry through for fear of death, the obstructions are multiplied exceedingly. So it was with us. Of its total length of sixty miles, we did the first part, or forty miles, straight off without any delay, passing the well-known halting-places of our army in 1838—Siri Bolan, a spot only seventy to eighty feet broad, with steep cliffs on each side, Qutlgah, Abigoom, Rood Bahar, to Beebee Nanee, then on to Kirtah, the only village in the Pass. Here I halted, having been sixteen hours in the saddle, and, thanks to God, we were providentially saved from encountering any of the beasts of prey, in the shape of man, that infest the Pass—and the narrows of Beebee Nanee, with its precipitous rocks, were safely got through. Its high, water-worn cliffs, full of large caves, overhang the road in such a manner, that stones let fall from above would kill any one passing below. Here a few resolute men could stop the advance of a large force; and in the spot where the stream cuts through the hill and debouches into the small plain of Kirtah, the valley is only three hundred yards broad, and the road is of deep loose shingle, very difficult to travel on. The village is inhabited by Koochak Beloochees.

The next day we started late from this poor little village, over a road worse if possible than yesterday, being formed of pointed limestone boulders and rocks, and which follows the windings of the stream, which we crossed and recrossed a dozen times, the water reaching up to our saddle flaps; but in the months of July, August, and September this road is at its worst, owing to the rains that fall then, and the deep water in the river, making it a very difficult one for a heavily-laden caravan.

The tribe of Murrees who usually closed the Pass have their villages nearly thirty miles off, yet they come down and commit all the excesses for which this place has become noted. As we neared the town of Dadur, the Pass opened out and merged into the plain; the road still followed the river, and when we arrived in sight of the town I sent on a man to give information of my arrival. After an hour's rest on the banks of the stream I again advanced, and when close to the town met the Dadur Naib's son, with some Beloochees, who escorted me into the small town, which has a fort and a mud wall, and is situated on the left bank of the Bolan stream: it is a place of some importance, and consequently gave me a noisy reception. Here I heard that the political agent to the Khan of Khelat, the Chief of the Beloochees, was encamped close by, to whom I wrote, and in answer he kindly invited me to breakfast. So on the next day I rode into Bagh on a camel, behind the Naib's son, where I found the Khan of Khelat and his army, likewise the agent, Major Harrison, all in camp. He kindly gave me a tent, and made me comfortable.

I cannot describe the pleasure I felt in again being with my countrymen, and able to converse in my own tongue. After staying two days with the Major and his companion the Doctor, I started for Jocobabad, our frontier station in Sind. The road lays over the Put, a dreary plain, which was very slippery from the rain that had lately fallen; we saw a mirage on all sides. Having been hospitably entertained by the officers of the Sind Horse at

Jocobabad, I reached Shikarpore and Sukker on the 10th January, 1873.

Having come to the end of my journey, I only wish to add a few notes. The approximate distances crossed were:—

From Enzeli to Teheran	200	miles.
„ Teheran to Meshed	550	„
„ Meshed to Herat	230	„
„ Herat to Candahar	400	„
„ Candahar to Jacobabad	300	„
Total miles	1680	

the last nine hundred miles on one horse, the Turkoman I had purchased at Meshed.

This route, of course, is well known. My only idea in traversing it was to become acquainted with a road which may before long be of the utmost importance to us. The Eastern Question will not be settled by the taking of Khiva by the Russians, and no neutral zone will protect us from, at least, the inconvenience of intrigues between Russia and Afghanistan. "Out of sight out of mind" is an old saying, but I hope we shall not allow it to be proved. By our present policy we are hardly known in Central

Asia. Our commerce is very poor; and not till the "personal influence" of our Agents and Politicals at Herat, Candahar, Balkh, and Cabul, also in Yarkund, is felt, will our former prestige revive, and that of Russia diminish. However large, as a theatre, Asia is, it appears not large enough for two such actors. Adieu, "Khoda Hafiz!"

24th May, 1873.—Since writing the above, time has brought about the solution of the last act in the Central Asiatic drama. "Khiva" has fallen, and not only fallen, but has also been annexed to Russia. The Ameer of Bokhara has been sent out of his city of Bokhara to live at Samarcand, so as not to interfere with the Russian government of the country. A large tract of country has also been wrested from Persia along the south-east shores of the Caspian, of which Krasnovodsk and Chikishlar are the most important places. As "Kokan" has not yet actually been taken, we only hear of a road being made to the capital, and a Russian agent being permanently settled there, and disturbances commencing, which is, of course, the thin end of the wedge. The country of the Atalikh Ghazee of Yarkund is virtually free. Russian merchandise is to be allowed to circulate freely through his country at a minimum tariff; also a road fit for wheel traffic has been constructed to within 150 miles of Kashgar—that is, near Fort Narayn; and we hear that a Russian agent is to be allowed to live in Yarkund, under the protection of its ruler.

June, 1874.—Lastly, we have the Cabul Ameer taking the birthright from his eldest son, Yakoob, and giving it to the youngest, Abdool Jan; also an embassy has been sent by Shere Ali to Bokhara, to congratulate the Russian Government on the capture of Khiva, in August, 1873.

Little by little we have been pushed out of the way by the aggression of a gigantic State. Our prestige and position with respect to Central Asian affairs has slowly, but surely, been dimmed and driven back. If, as some say, it is better to have a Christian and civilised neighbour, instead of savages, we must thoroughly understand that, in the first case, we are being bound by iron bonds which we may hereafter feel to be most oppressive; but that, in the second case, we might have had a very wide area wherein to exert our influence, and to construct for ourselves a political and commercial frontier unassailable to influence foreign to our own. But as our policy has allowed Russia to approach and nearly surround us, we ought to be more jealous of the only two countries left us to expand in—viz., Afghanistan and Yarkund. We want no extension of territory, only that of influence and commerce. Thanks to Sir Douglas Forsyth's energy and tact, Yarkund has been opened to us. When will Afghan exclusion be a thing of the past? Surely we ought to be allowed a free passage, after having given Shere Ali, since 1868, some fourteen lakhs of money,* twelve guns, thirteen to fourteen thousand stand of arms, besides elephants, ammunition, &c.

* £140,000.

CONCLUSION.

July, 1877.

THE events in which the British people are chiefly interested in Central Asia are brought about by the rapid advance of Russian arms and influence; and since the date of my last note of June, 1874, news from those parts does not show that the Czar's officers have relaxed any of their former zeal and activity in extending the boundaries of his vast dominions. First we received information that a rebellion had broken out in Kokand against Khodayar Khan, a chief who had been raised to the throne by the Russians; so that during 1875, after a gallant struggle, the indigenous forces were by degrees defeated and dispersed, and in January, 1876, the Imperial ukase decreed the annexation of the whole Khanate of Kokand—thus advancing the Russian frontier to the crests of the Alai and Kashgar Dewan mountains.

We must consider what this means. By this conquest the Russian frontier has been advanced towards the south *until it has reached to seventy-five miles only, in a straight line, from the northern frontier of Afghanistan, the Oxus River.* This river is the boundary over which the Russians must not pass, and to this our Government has pledged itself. Then, again, this annexation has brought Russia face to face with the Amir of Kashgar, in whose welfare and independence we have the greatest interest; in fact, the Russians are nearer to him than we are, as their outposts overlook his territory, but we are separated by three lofty ranges of mountains, communications through which are of the most difficult character. The taking of this last surviving Khanate also brings the Russians indirectly into contact with Afghanistan along the whole of her northern border—because the small States of Hissar, Kabadian, Kolab, Karatigin, Darwaz, &c., are claimed by the Russians as dependencies of their former conquest, Bokhara, or of Kokand. Formerly these petty chiefships were comparatively unknown, but in 1874–5 the whole of these countries were surveyed and explored by the Russians, so that the seventy-five miles before alluded to have been bridged over, and now it only remains for the Czar to annex them by ukase.

This conquest also affects that large tract of elevated plateaux, the Pamir. It has been lately discovered that these plains offer no physical difficulties during the summer months to being traversed in any direction. In 1876 a Russian armed expedition, sent against some nomadic Kirgiz from Kokand, penetrated up to its centre, the Uzbel Pass, south of Lake Karakul, and about ninety miles in a direct line from the northern frontier of Wakhan, which is a part of Afghanistan; and about 200 miles by the road from the Burogil Pass, at the head of the Kunr valley, which will be the road of the future into Central Asia. The Burogil, is by road about 320 miles, *viâ* Jellalabad, and the Khyber or Tatara Passes to Peshawur. The Russians have already established a military post on the Kizilsue,* beyond the frontier of annexed Kokand, and have taxed the Kirgiz on the Pamir—so that, with the present exception of the two petty States of Roshan and Shignan, to the east of Budukshan, we may say Russian influence extends along our northern frontiers from longitude 75° to 65° at Khoja Sala, on the Oxus.

* On the Pamir.

The formation of the Trans-Caspian province in 1874, to the east of the Caspian, at the expense of Persia, our ally, opens out the road to Merv. Several expeditions have advanced in that direction, conquering the Western Turkoman tribes, but have not penetrated further than Beurma, in longitude 57°; but we have lately received reports that a force is being massed at Chardjui, on the Oxus, only 150 miles by road from Killa Nau, the fort of Merv. If Merv is taken by the Russians, it will at once threaten Persia and Afghanistan.

The province of Kashgar, formed only twelve years ago by the present Amir, Yakoob Ali,* at the expense of China, holds the same position on our north-east as Afghanistan does to our north-western frontier. The Kashgar Amir has formed a treaty with the Russians, which permits a Russian officer to reside at his Court, and grants them every facility for their commerce; *these privileges are also extended to us, but we have no permanent resident there.* Russia has acknowledged the independence of this State, and has declared she has no desire to interfere with its

* Now dead, and has been succeeded by his son.

liberty. If this "fair field and no favour" policy could be depended on, we should have nothing to fear—but a danger looms in the distance, of which we can at present say little. China has declared her determination to reconquer her lost province of Kashgar, and for the last three years her army has been slowly marching up through the province of Kansu and retaking her own; and quite recently we hear that the Amir's forces have been defeated and forced to retire from Turfan to Kuchar, in latitude 41°·40, and longitude 82°·80; but, as an army of locusts, the Chinese are still advancing to take Aksu, still further to the west. The Russians will, of course, be only too well pleased at this advance of the Chinese, as they will be freer in future to treat China as they may find convenient; while at present Kashgar is looked upon as rather under our protection.

Finally, we must not speak decidedly on the agitation at present caused by the Russo-Turkish war among the Mahomedans throughout Islam; but if we find them joining together and working in unison against Russia, we must expect the followers of the Prophet in India some day, in a like manner, uniting against us—so that the problem of our holding India to our advantage becomes more difficult to solve. India can hardly afford to keep the present force of 60,000 British bayonets; and if more have to be added to enable us to keep our hold on the country, we shall have to tax the population still more, which might be hazardous, as education is increasing the power of the masses, and they are asserting their independence more vigorously year by year. The advance of Russia and her civilisation might have been more acceptable to us if she had been an advocate for free trade, but we know by experience her way of working—prohibitive tariffs, despotism, and curtailment of religious liberty—so that with these in view, no Englishman can look with indifference at the present aspect of affairs in the East. To preserve internal tranquillity and progress in India, we *must interfere* in the politics of Persia, Afghanistan, Kashgar, and the small States north of the Oxus* and Indus,† to the exclusion of Russian interests, prestige, or intrigue. But to accomplish this effectually, we must remain within our present boundaries;

* Kolab, Darwaz, Roshan, Shignan.

† Kunjut, Yassin, Chitral, Kaffiristan, or, collectively, Yaghistan.

any annexation on our part will undo the effects of the policy of the last twenty-five years. Ever since the Cabul campaign we have been endeavouring to allay the fears of our jealous neighbours, by not advancing our frontier under any circumstances. If we follow this policy we shall be acting consistently, and with greater freedom be able to extend our interests, commercially and politically, without encountering the hostility of our Mahomedan neighbours. With these views, I consider the occupation of Quetta by our native troops as a false move; but if they were withdrawn and a Political Officer be established permanently at the Court of the Khan of Kelat, we should enjoy all the advantages of a spirited move, without any of its drawbacks.

NOTES.

Note 1, Page 11.

Considering how large a stake British capitalists have in most of the ports of the Levant and Black Sea, also in the Red Sea, Persian Gulf, and other parts of Asia, I am surprised that our interests are so often, or rather, as a rule, intrusted to the care of those who are not Englishmen. Any small local merchant—very often not even a British subject—is now thought capable of representing us, and protecting our trade and the persons of British-born subjects. The suggestion I have often heard advanced, that we should have a regular Consular College to train Englishmen for these important posts, is one of vast importance, and deserves the serious attention of our Government.

Note 2, Page 54.

This material, as fuel for the furnaces of steamers, is receiving considerable attention at present, but, owing to its dangerous qualities, difficulties have presented themselves, which, together with prejudice, have prevented this natural product, of which there is an abundant supply, not only here,* but also in America and Burmah, from being utilised to the extent it deserves; although, for warming houses and for cooking purposes, stoves burning earth oils have found favour throughout the world.

Note 3, Page 58.

In the year 1836 the whole of the Caspian Sea was, by treaty, closed to Persia, her boatmen, and her trade. About the same

* Baku.

year Russia first set her eyes on Ashuradé, an island situated at the end of a spit of land jutting out of the Mazenderan coast, and sheltering the only safe and deep harbour on the south-east of the Caspian; but it was not till 1841-3 that the island was regularly seized and the foundation laid for the formation of a naval station. This flagrant robbery caused a slight remonstrance to be addressed to Russia by the British Government at the earnest solicitations of Persia; but the demand for restitution not having been enforced, ended by the Russians strengthening their hold on the island, notwithstanding that, in 1854, Persia again officially demanded its evacuation, and about the same time Russia forced her Consuls on Persia, and established them at Resht and Astrabad. In like manner, in 1869, Krasnovodsk, and in 1871 Chikishlår and the neighbouring coasts, were seized—Persia protesting, and we silently watching the spoliation!

THE END.